Better Homes and Gardens®

SMOKE
Cooking

Better Homes and Gardens® Books
Des Moines, Iowa

Copyright © 2001 by
Meredith Corporation, Des Moines, Iowa.
All rights reserved.
Printed in China.
First Edition—00
Library of Congress
Catalog Control Number: 00-136443
ISBN: 0-696-21356-7

Pictured on front cover: Texas-Style Beef Ribs, page 20
Cover photo: Pete Krumhardt, Photographer; Janet Pittman, Food Stylist

Better Homes and Gardens® Books
An imprint of Meredith® Books

Smoke Cooking
Editor: Jan Miller, R.D.
Contributing Editor: Spectrum Communication Services, Inc.
Contributing Writer: Lisa Kingsley
Associate Art Director: Lynda Haupert
Copy Chief: Catherine Hamrick
Copy and Production Editor: Terri Fredrickson
Managers, Book Production: Pam Kvitne, Marjorie J. Schenkelberg
Contributing Copy Editor: Sheila Mauck
Contributing Proofreaders: Gretchen Kauffman, Susan J. Kling, Margaret Smith
Electronic Production Coordinator: Paula Forest
Editorial and Design Assistants: Judy Bailey, Mary Lee Gavin, Karen Schirm
Test Kitchen Director: Lynn Blanchard
Test Kitchen Product Supervisor: Marilyn Cornelius
Test Kitchen Home Economists: Judy Comstock, Maryellyn Krantz, Tami Leonard, Jill Lust, Jill Moberly, Dianna Nolin, Kay Springer, Colleen Weeden, Lori Wilson, Charles Worthington

Meredith® Books
Editor in Chief: James D. Blume
Design Director: Matt Strelecki
Managing Editor: Gregory H. Kayko
Executive Food Editor: Jennifer Dorland Darling

Director, Retail Sales and Marketing: Terry Unsworth
Director, Sales, Special Markets: Rita McMullen
Director, Sales, Premiums: Michael A. Peterson
Director, Sales, Retail: Tom Wierzbicki
Director, Book Marketing: Brad Elmitt
Director, Operations: George A. Susral
Director, Production: Douglas M. Johnston

Vice President, General Manager: Jamie L. Martin

Better Homes and Gardens® Magazine
Editor in Chief: Jean LemMon
Executive Food Editor: Nancy Byal

Meredith Publishing Group
President, Publishing Group: Stephen M. Lacy
Vice President, Finance and Administration: Max Runciman

Meredith Corporation
Chairman and Chief Executive Officer: William T. Kerr

Chairman of the Executive Committee: E. T. Meredith III

Contents

Welcome to Our Kitchen

When you cook with a Better Homes and Gardens® cookbook, you can be confident that every recipe will taste great every time. That's because we perfect each recipe in our Test Kitchen before we present it to you.

Few things are more enticing than the smell of barbecue smoke drifting across a beautiful sunny afternoon. It's enough to make your mouth water.

The Home Economists in the Better Homes and Gardens® Test Kitchen spent many smoky afternoons ensuring that each recipe in *Smoke Cooking* is successful for the novice and pro alike. The recipes in *Smoke Cooking* are written for either a smoker or a grill. No matter the method, they are all easy, no-fail, and full of great, smoky taste.

We share the most important techniques of smoke cooking in Secrets to Success and pass along plenty of tips throughout the book. You'll find helpful information on such topics as smoke cooking safety, how to pair types of wood with food for optimum flavor, and how to keep your smoke sweet. If you're looking for low-fat recipes, look for ♥. This symbol identifies main-dish recipes with 10 grams or less of total fat.

If you're feeling creative, use the smoke-cooking timing charts on the inside front and back covers. These charts make it easy to design your own recipe by pairing your favorite meat, poultry, fish, or seafood with a sauce from "Sauces, Rubs & Marinades."

On the days we're baking, roasting, or stewing in the Test Kitchen, a few visitors wander in, drawn by the aromas. On the days we smoke cook, we attract lots of company. If you don't happen to have an authentic barbecue shack in the neighborhood, *Smoke Cooking* helps you create one right in your own backyard. If you haven't yet become acquainted with your neighbors, get ready to make some new friends.

Lynn Blanchard

Lynn Blanchard
Better Homes and Gardens®
Test Kitchen Director

Secrets to Success

Although smoke cooking is an ancient art, it's new to many cooks. The Better Homes and Gardens® Test Kitchen Home Economists receive lots of questions about the method. If they don't have an answer, they research it until they do. Here are their answers to the most common questions.

Q.

Are there different types of smokers?

A.

Yes, and they all give the same moist, tender, smoky results. The three main types of smokers are charcoal, electric, and gas. The only difference is the source of their heat. Most of the smokers purchased for home use are charcoal vertical water smokers, meaning the cylindrical cookers stand upright and contain a water pan that creates a moist heat as the food cooks. (Dry smokers are usually horizontal units with an offset firebox that keeps the food away from the heat source; as their name implies, they do not contain a water pan.) A very simple charcoal water smoker can be purchased for as little as $60. One advantage of charcoal smokers is that they're portable—they can be taken picnicking, camping, or tailgating. The greatest advantage of electric or gas smokers is that they easily maintain a constant temperature ideal for smoke cooking. Electric smokers can simply be plugged into an outdoor outlet.

Q.

How does a water smoker work?

A.

A water smoker uses the heat from hot coals to bring the water in the pan to boiling while causing the soaked wood chunks to begin smoking. The water particles unite with the smoke particles, which then condense on the meat. This creates three desirable effects: The meat is infused with a delicious, sweet smoke flavor; it gets tenderized; and it remains moist despite a long cooking time. The water vapor also helps keep the temperature in the chamber hovering between 200° and 275°—ideal for smoke cooking. When you're lighting the coals in your smoker, be sure the vents are wide open to allow the coals to catch fire. For smoking, all of the vents should be partially closed. Refer to the manufacturer's directions for specific instructions about using your smoke cooker.

Q.

If I don't own a smoker, can I still make smoked foods on my grill?

A.

Absolutely. Whether you own a charcoal or gas grill, you can smoke foods on your grill by using the indirect method of grilling—meaning the food is cooked adjacent to the heat source rather than directly over it—and by adding soaked hardwood chips to the hot coals or heating element. To set up a charcoal grill for indirect cooking, light the coals. Arrange glowing coals around the grill perimeter using long-handle tongs. When the coals are covered with gray ash, set a drip pan in the center of the grill, surrounded by coals, directly under where the food will be placed. To check the temperature over the drip pan, hold your hand where the food will cook for as long as it's comfortable. For our recipes, a hot fire allows a 2-second hand count, a medium fire allows a 4-second count and a low fire allows a 6-second hand count.

Indirect grilling on a gas grill takes even less preparation. Light the grill according to the manufacturer's instructions. Turn the setting to high, and let the grill preheat for 10 to 15 minutes. Reduce the heat on one burner to medium or medium-high, and turn the other burner off to set up two heat zones. Place the drip pan directly on the lava rocks, ceramic briquettes, or flavorizer bars on the burner that's turned off. Adjust the gas flow to the burner that's on to maintain the desired temperature inside the firebox. Check the temperature over the drip pan as described above. Place the food on the grill rack directly over the drip pan.

Q.

How do I keep a constant temperature while I smoke cook?

A.

Smoke cooking often requires leisurely cooking times. To make sure the coals stay hot enough to keep the wood smoking, add no more than 10 to 12 charcoal briquettes every hour or so. Adding too many coals at once causes the temperature in the chamber to plummet. If you are smoke cooking on your grill, add half of the new coals to each side. If your fire is medium hot and the coals are burning quickly, you may need to add a few briquettes as often as every 30 minutes. Add soaked wood chunks or chips as often as necessary to maintain a steady source of smoke. If you need to add water to the pan, make sure it is hot water so the temperature in the chamber doesn't fluctuate greatly. And though it's tempting to peek at what you're cooking, resist the urge to lift the lid of your smoker or grill. Every time you do, you'll need to add 15 minutes to the cooking time.

Beef & Lamb

Brisket with 5-Alarm Sauce

In This Chapter:

Herbed Rib Roast with Dijon Sauce

This Dijon-sauced rib roast—sometimes labeled as standing rib roast or beef prime rib—is elegant enough for the most demanding dinner guests.

Prep: 20 minutes **Marinate:** 2 hours **Smoke:** 2 hours **Stand:** 15 minutes **Serves:** 8

1 4-pound beef rib roast

Marinade:

¾ cup dry red wine

½ cup finely chopped onion

¼ cup lemon juice

¼ cup water

1 tablespoon Worcestershire sauce

½ teaspoon dried rosemary, crushed

½ teaspoon dried marjoram, crushed

¼ teaspoon garlic salt

4 cups hickory or mesquite wood chips

Sauce:

1 8-ounce carton dairy sour cream

2 tablespoons Dijon-style mustard

½ teaspoon lemon-pepper seasoning

1 Trim fat from meat. Place meat in a plastic bag set in a shallow dish. For marinade, in a medium bowl combine wine, onion, lemon juice, water, Worcestershire sauce, rosemary, marjoram, and garlic salt. Pour over meat; seal bag. Marinate in the refrigerator for 2 to 6 hours, turning bag occasionally.

2 At least 1 hour before smoke cooking, soak wood chips in enough water to cover. Drain before using. Drain meat, reserving marinade. Insert a meat thermometer into center of meat without touching bone.

3 *In a charcoal grill*, arrange medium coals around a drip pan. Test for medium-low heat above the pan. Sprinkle half of the drained wood chips over the coals. Place meat, fat side up, on the grill rack over drip pan. Cover and smoke until meat thermometer registers 140° for medium-rare (2 to 2½ hours) or 155° for medium doneness (2½ to 3 hours), brushing once with marinade halfway through cooking. Add more coals and wood chips as needed. [*In a gas grill*, preheat grill. Reduce heat to medium-low. Adjust for indirect cooking (see page 6). Add drained wood chips according to the manufacturer's directions. Smoke as above, except place meat, fat side up, on a rack in a roasting pan.] Discard the remaining marinade.

4 Meanwhile, for sauce, in a small bowl combine sour cream, mustard, and lemon-pepper seasoning. Cover and refrigerate until ready to serve.

5 Remove meat from grill. Cover meat with foil; let stand for 15 minutes before carving. (The meat's temperature will rise 5° during standing.) To serve, slice the meat and serve with sauce.

Nutrition Facts per serving: 244 cal., 13 g total fat (6 g sat. fat), 64 mg chol., 229 mg sodium, 4 g carbo., 0 g fiber, 23 g pro.
Daily Values: 5% vit. A, 8% vit. C, 6% calcium, 12% iron

Mesquite-Smoked Beef Roast ♥ SMOKER

Serve leftovers of this smoky beef roast cold and sliced thin on toasted sourdough bread with a slather of cilantro, chipotle, or jalapeño mayonnaise, and slivers of roasted red peppers.

Soak: 1 hour **Prep:** 10 minutes **Smoke:** 3 hours **Stand:** 15 minutes **Serves:** 12

8 to 10 mesquite or hickory wood chunks
1 4-pound boneless beef rib eye roast
   Whole black peppercorns

Rub:
1½ teaspoons Worcestershire sauce
½ teaspoon seasoned salt
½ teaspoon celery salt

1 At least 1 hour before smoke cooking, soak wood chunks in enough water to cover. Drain before using.

2 Trim fat from meat. Using a long-tined fork, make holes about ¾ inch apart and 1 inch deep on top side of meat; insert a whole peppercorn into each hole. Close holes by rubbing the surface of the meat with the smooth edge of the fork.

3 For rub, in a small bowl combine Worcestershire sauce, seasoned salt, and celery salt. Drizzle mixture evenly over meat; rub in with your fingers. Insert a meat thermometer into the center of meat.

4 *In a smoker,* arrange preheated coals, half of the drained wood chunks, and the water pan according to the manufacturer's directions. Pour water into pan. Place meat on the grill rack over water pan. Cover and smoke until meat thermometer registers 140° for medium-rare doneness (3 to 3½ hours). Add more coals, wood chunks, and water as needed.

5 Remove meat from smoker. Cover meat with foil; let stand for 15 minutes before carving. (The meat's temperature will rise 5° during standing.)

Nutrition Facts per serving: 226 cal., 9 g total fat (4 g sat. fat), 71 mg chol., 216 mg sodium, 0 g carbo., 0 g fiber, 33 g pro.
Daily Values: 1% calcium, 16% iron

Marinated Rump Roast ♥

The vinegar in the marinade for this classic barbecue recipe works wonders on the flavor and texture of the meat. Along with the spices, it gives the roast tongue-tingling flavor and tenderizes it to boot.

Prep: 20 minutes **Marinate:** 24 hours **Smoke:** 1½ hours **Stand:** 15 minutes **Serves:** 12

1 3-pound boneless beef
   rump roast, rolled
   and tied

Marinade:

2½ cups water
2½ cups vinegar
 2 medium onions, sliced
 1 medium lemon, sliced
 2 or 3 bay leaves
12 whole cloves
 6 whole black peppercorns
 1 teaspoon salt

 4 cups mesquite, hickory, or
    oak wood chips

1 Trim fat from meat. Place meat in a plastic bag set in a deep, large bowl. For marinade, in a medium bowl combine water, vinegar, onions, lemon, bay leaves, cloves, peppercorns, and salt. Pour over meat; seal bag. Marinate in the refrigerator for 24 hours, turning bag occasionally.

2 At least 1 hour before smoke cooking, soak wood chips in enough water to cover. Drain before using. Drain meat, reserving marinade. Insert a meat thermometer into center of meat.

3 *In a charcoal grill*, arrange medium coals around a drip pan. Test for medium-low heat above the pan. Sprinkle half of the drained wood chips over the coals. Place meat on the grill rack over drip pan. Cover and smoke until meat thermometer registers 155° for medium doneness (1½ to 2 hours), brushing once with marinade halfway through cooking. Add more coals and wood chips as needed. [*In a gas grill*, preheat grill. Reduce heat to medium-low. Adjust for indirect cooking (see page 6). Add drained wood chips according to the manufacturer's directions. Smoke as above, except place meat on a rack in a roasting pan.] Discard the remaining marinade.

4 Remove meat from grill. Cover meat with foil; let stand for 15 minutes before carving. (The meat's temperature will rise 5° during standing.)

Nutrition Facts per serving: 155 cal., 4 g total fat (1 g sat. fat), 60 mg chol., 129 mg sodium, 1 g carbo., 0 g fiber, 25 g pro.
Daily Values: 1% vit. C, 1% calcium, 13% iron

Brisket with 5-Alarm Sauce ♥

Brisket—a cut not known for its submissive qualities—falls off the fork after 5 to 6 hours in the smoker and a good mopping with a spicy (not hot) sauce. Serve with grilled miniature sweet peppers.

Soak: 1 hour **Prep:** 15 minutes **Smoke:** 5 hours **Serves:** 12

8 to 10 mesquite or hickory wood chunks

Mop Sauce:
¼ cup dry red wine
4 teaspoons Worcestershire sauce
1 tablespoon cooking oil
1 tablespoon red wine vinegar or cider vinegar
1 clove garlic, minced
1 coriander seed, crushed
½ teaspoon hot-style mustard Dash ground red pepper

Rub:
2 teaspoons seasoned salt
1 teaspoon paprika
1 teaspoon black pepper

1 3- to 3½-pound fresh beef brisket
1 recipe 5-Alarm Sauce

1 At least 1 hour before smoke cooking, soak wood chunks in enough water to cover. Drain before using.

2 For mop sauce, in a small bowl combine wine, Worcestershire sauce, oil, vinegar, garlic, coriander seed, mustard, and ground red pepper. Set aside.

3 For rub, in a small bowl combine seasoned salt, paprika, and black pepper. Trim fat from meat. Sprinkle rub evenly over meat; rub in with your fingers.

4 *In a smoker*, arrange preheated coals, half of the drained wood chunks, and the water pan according to the manufacturer's directions. Pour water into pan. Place meat on the grill rack over water pan. Cover and smoke for 5 to 6 hours or until meat is tender, brushing once or twice with mop sauce during the last 1 hour of cooking. Add more coals, wood chunks, and water as needed. Discard any remaining mop sauce.

5 To serve, thinly slice meat across the grain. Serve meat with 5-Alarm Sauce.

5-Alarm Sauce: In a medium saucepan stir together 1 cup catsup; 1 large tomato, peeled, seeded, and chopped; 1 small green sweet pepper, chopped; 2 tablespoons brown sugar; 2 tablespoons chopped onion; 1 to 2 tablespoons steak sauce; 1 to 2 tablespoons Worcestershire sauce; ½ teaspoon garlic powder; ¼ teaspoon ground nutmeg; ¼ teaspoon ground cinnamon; ¼ teaspoon ground cloves; ⅛ teaspoon ground ginger; and ⅛ teaspoon black pepper. Bring to boiling; reduce heat. Cover and simmer about 5 minutes or until green pepper is crisp-tender. Serve warm or at room temperature. Makes about 2½ cups.

Nutrition Facts per serving: 214 cal., 8 g total fat (2 g sat. fat), 66 mg chol., 618 mg sodium, 10 g carbo., 1 g fiber, 25 g pro.
Daily Values: 9% vit. A, 21% vit. C, 2% calcium, 15% iron

Barbecued Beef Brisket ♥

A bottled sauce provides the base for this easy-to-make marinade and mop that's freshened up with onion, garlic, and—yes, that's right—coffee. Remember, barbecued brisket benefits from thin slicing.

Prep: 20 minutes **Marinate:** 6 hours **Smoke:** 2 hours **Serves:** 12

1 3- to 4-pound fresh beef brisket

Marinade:

½ cup water

½ cup bottled barbecue sauce

1 small onion, finely chopped

2 tablespoons Worcestershire sauce

1 tablespoon instant coffee crystals

1 tablespoon vinegar

1 tablespoon cooking oil

3 cloves garlic, minced

½ teaspoon seasoned pepper

4 cups hickory or mesquite wood chips

1 Trim fat from meat. Place meat in a plastic bag set in a shallow dish. For marinade, in a small bowl combine water, barbecue sauce, onion, Worcestershire sauce, coffee crystals, vinegar, cooking oil, garlic, and pepper. Pour over meat; seal bag. Marinate meat in the refrigerator for 6 to 24 hours, turning bag occasionally.

2 At least 1 hour before smoke cooking, soak wood chips in enough water to cover. Drain before using. Drain meat, reserving marinade.

3 *In a charcoal grill*, arrange medium-low coals around a drip pan. Test for low heat above the pan. Sprinkle half of the drained wood chips over the coals. Place meat on the grill rack over drip pan. Cover and smoke for 2 to 2½ hours or until meat is tender, brushing once with marinade halfway through cooking. Add more coals and wood chips as needed. [*In a gas grill*, preheat grill. Reduce heat to low. Adjust for indirect cooking (see page 6). Add drained wood chips according to the manufacturer's directions. Smoke as above, except place meat on a rack in a roasting pan.]

4 To serve, thinly slice meat across the grain. In a small saucepan bring the remaining marinade to boiling. Boil gently, uncovered, for 1 minute. Pass with meat.

Nutrition Facts per serving: 187 cal., 8 g total fat (2 g sat. fat), 66 mg chol., 185 mg sodium, 3 g carbo., 0 g fiber, 25 g pro.
Daily Values: 2% vit. A, 3% vit. C, 1% calcium, 14% iron

Lemon-Basil Steaks SMOKER

Balsamic vinegar adds a rich mahogany color and a malty sweetness to the glaze on these rib eyes. Serve the steaks with potato salad and crusty sourdough bread.

Soak: 1 hour **Prep:** 5 minutes **Smoke:** 40 minutes **Serves:** 4

4 hickory, pecan, or oak wood chunks

Glaze:
2 teaspoons country-style Dijon-style mustard
2 teaspoons balsamic vinegar
1½ teaspoons lemon-pepper seasoning
2 cloves garlic, minced
1 teaspoon dried basil, crushed
⅛ teaspoon salt

4 boneless beef rib eye steaks, cut 1 inch thick (1¾ to 2 pounds total)

1 At least 1 hour before smoke cooking, soak wood chunks in enough water to cover. Drain before using.

2 For glaze, in a small bowl stir together mustard, vinegar, lemon-pepper seasoning, garlic, basil, and salt. Trim fat from steaks. Brush glaze onto both sides of steaks.

3 *In a smoker,* arrange preheated coals, drained wood chunks, and water pan according to the manufacturer's directions. Pour water into water pan. Place steaks on the grill rack over pan. Cover and smoke until steaks are desired doneness. (Allow 40 to 50 minutes for medium-rare or 50 to 60 minutes for medium doneness.)

Nutrition Facts per serving: 307 cal., 12 g total fat (5 g sat. fat), 94 mg chol., 599 mg sodium, 2 g carbo., 0 g fiber, 44 g pro.
Daily Values: 1% vit. C, 3% calcium, 22% iron

Steak with Olive Relish

If you like the rich, meaty flavor of kalamata olives, substitute them for the plain ripe olives in this Mediterranean-style relish. The relish would also be right at home atop grilled Italian bread.

Prep: 15 minutes **Chill:** 2 hours **Smoke:** 16 minutes **Serves:** 4

Relish:

- 1   6½-ounce jar marinated artichoke hearts
- 2   medium tomatoes, peeled, seeded, and chopped (1 cup)
- 1   cup pitted ripe olives, halved lengthwise
- ¼   cup thinly sliced green onions
- 1   tablespoon red wine vinegar
- 1   clove garlic, minced
- ⅛   teaspoon pepper

- 2   cups oak or hickory wood chips
- 4   boneless beef top loin steaks, cut 1 inch thick (1¾ to 2 pounds total)
- 2   to 4 teaspoons steak seasoning

1 For relish, drain artichokes, reserving marinade. Coarsely chop artichokes. In a medium bowl combine artichokes, reserved marinade, tomatoes, olives, green onions, vinegar, garlic, and pepper. Cover and refrigerate for 2 to 4 hours to blend flavors.

2 At least 1 hour before smoke cooking, soak wood chips in enough water to cover. Drain before using. Trim fat from steaks. Sprinkle steak seasoning evenly over steaks; rub in with your fingers.

3 *In a charcoal grill,* arrange medium-hot coals around a drip pan. Test for medium heat above the pan. Sprinkle the drained wood chips over the coals. Place steaks on the grill rack over drip pan. Cover and smoke until steaks are desired doneness. (Allow 16 to 20 minutes for medium-rare or 20 to 24 minutes for medium doneness.) [*In a gas grill,* preheat grill. Reduce heat to medium. Adjust for indirect cooking (see page 6). Smoke as above, except add drained wood chips according to the manufacturer's directions.] Serve the steaks with relish.

Nutrition Facts per serving: 490 cal., 32 g total fat (11 g sat. fat), 127 mg chol., 615 mg sodium, 10 g carbo., 2 g fiber, 41 g pro.
Daily Values: 9% vit. A, 34% vit. C, 7% calcium, 28% iron

Smoky Pepper Steaks SMOKER

This recipe offers peppery proof that in the world of barbecue, smoke is king. Chipotle peppers—smoked jalapeños—are sold both dried and canned in adobo sauce.

Soak: 1 hour **Prep:** 5 minutes **Smoke:** 40 minutes **Serves:** 4

4 pecan, oak, or hickory wood chunks

Glaze:

2 to 4 tablespoons finely chopped chipotle peppers in adobo sauce
2 tablespoons lime juice
2 tablespoons cooking oil
4 cloves garlic, minced
¼ teaspoon salt

4 boneless beef top loin steaks, cut 1 inch thick (1¾ to 2 pounds total)

1 At least 1 hour before smoke cooking, soak wood chunks in enough water to cover. Drain before using.

2 For glaze, in a small bowl stir together chipotle peppers in sauce, lime juice, cooking oil, garlic, and salt. Trim fat from steaks. Brush glaze onto both sides of steaks.

3 *In a smoker,* arrange preheated coals, drained wood chunks, and water pan according to the manufacturer's directions. Pour water into pan. Place steaks on the grill rack over water pan. Cover and smoke until steaks are desired doneness. (Allow 40 to 50 minutes for medium-rare or 50 to 60 minutes for medium doneness.)

Nutrition Facts per serving: 467 cal., 32 g total fat (11 g sat. fat), 126 mg chol., 317 mg sodium, 3 g carbo., 0 g fiber, 39 g pro.
Daily Values: 6% vit. C, 2% calcium, 19% iron

safe smoke cooking

Smoking is a perfectly pleasant and enjoyable way to cook if you follow a few simple rules:

• Never use a smoker or outdoor-type grill indoors—not even in the garage.

• Set up your smoker or grill in as windless a condition as possible, as far from your house as possible. The scent of wood smoke tends to linger.

• Never use a smoker or grill on a wooden deck or near flammable material.

• Never use charcoal that already has starter fluid in it in a smoker. Use lump hardwood charcoal or, if your smoker works best with briquettes, seek out those made from natural materials such as nuts and vegetable starches.

Steak Strips with Peanut Sauce

Nothing could be simpler and more satisfying than this four-ingredient peanut sauce that's stirred together on top of the stove. Serve the steak and sauce with hot cooked rice.

Prep: 15 minutes **Marinate:** 4 hours **Smoke:** 22 minutes **Serves:** 8

1 2-pound boneless beef sirloin steak, cut 1 inch thick

Marinade:
¼ cup unsweetened pineapple juice
2 tablespoons cooking oil
1 tablespoon lemon juice
1 teaspoon grated fresh ginger
1 teaspoon Dijon-style mustard

2 cups fruitwood chips

Sauce:
¼ cup creamy peanut butter
¼ to ⅓ cup unsweetened pineapple juice
1 to 2 tablespoons chopped, seeded fresh jalapeño pepper
1 small green onion, chopped
½ teaspoon grated fresh ginger (optional)

1 Trim fat from steak. Place steak in a plastic bag set in a shallow dish. For marinade, in a small bowl combine the ¼ cup pineapple juice, the cooking oil, lemon juice, the 1 teaspoon ginger, and the mustard. Pour over steak; seal bag. Marinate in the refrigerator for 4 to 24 hours, turning bag occasionally.

2 At least 1 hour before smoke cooking, soak wood chips in enough water to cover. Drain before using. Drain steak, reserving marinade.

3 *In a charcoal grill*, arrange medium-hot coals around a drip pan. Test for medium heat above the pan. Sprinkle the drained wood chips over the coals. Place steak on the grill rack over drip pan. Cover and smoke until steak is desired doneness, brushing once with marinade halfway through cooking. (Allow 22 to 26 minutes for medium-rare or 26 to 30 minutes for medium doneness.) [*In a gas grill*, preheat grill. Reduce heat to medium. Adjust for indirect cooking (see page 6). Smoke as above, except add drained wood chips according to the manufacturer's directions.] Discard the remaining marinade.

4 Meanwhile, for sauce, in a small saucepan heat peanut butter over low heat just until melted. Gradually stir in the ¼ to ⅓ cup pineapple juice until creamy (peanut butter mixture may thicken at first but will become creamy as more juice is added). Remove from heat. Stir in jalapeño pepper, green onion, and, if desired, the ½ teaspoon ginger.

5 To serve, thinly slice steak across the grain. Serve steak with sauce. If desired, garnish with additional green onion.

Nutrition Facts per serving: 233 cal., 12 g total fat (3 g sat. fat), 69 mg chol., 97 mg sodium, 4 g carbo., 1 g fiber, 26 g pro.
Daily Values: 6% vit. C, 2% calcium, 17% iron

Sirloin with Horseradish Sauce SMOKER

English cooks produced a winning dish in the classic chophouse combination of beef and horseradish. Here, the pair is at the top of its form as a smoky sirloin gilded with a silky horseradish sauce.

Prep: 15 minutes **Marinate:** 1 hour **Smoke:** 2 hours **Serves:** 6

Rub:

4 cloves garlic, minced
¾ teaspoon ground cumin
½ teaspoon cracked black pepper
¼ teaspoon salt

1 2- to 2½-pound beef sirloin steak, cut 1½ inches thick
6 to 8 oak or hickory wood chunks

Sauce:

⅓ cup dairy sour cream
2 tablespoons Dijon-style mustard
1 tablespoon snipped fresh chives
2 teaspoons prepared horseradish
¼ cup whipping cream, whipped

1 For rub, in a small bowl combine garlic, cumin, pepper, and salt. Trim fat from steak. Place steak in a shallow dish. Sprinkle rub evenly over one side of steak; rub in with your fingers. Cover and marinate in the refrigerator for 1 to 4 hours.

2 At least 1 hour before smoke cooking, soak wood chunks in enough water to cover. Drain before using.

3 *In a smoker*, arrange preheated coals, half of the drained wood chunks, and the water pan according to the manufacturer's directions. Pour water into pan. Place steak, seasoned side up, on the grill rack over water pan. Cover and smoke until steak is desired doneness. (Allow about 2 hours for medium-rare or about 2½ hours for medium doneness.) Add more coals, wood chunks, and water as needed.

4 Meanwhile, for sauce, in a small bowl combine sour cream, mustard, chives, and horseradish. Fold in whipped cream.

5 To serve, thinly slice steak across the grain. Pass the sauce with steak.

Nutrition Facts per serving: 261 cal., 13 g total fat (6 g sat. fat), 110 mg chol., 212 mg sodium, 2 g carbo., 0 g fiber, 33 g pro.
Daily Values: 5% vit. A, 2% vit. C, 4% calcium, 23% iron

Ginger-Orange Beef Ribs   SMOKER

Soy sauce and fresh ginger give these meaty ribs Pacific-Rim flair. An Asian cook might smoke them in a kamado, an egg-shape ceramic oven used for smoking in that part of the world for centuries.

Soak: 1 hour **Prep:** 10 minutes **Smoke:** 2½ hours **Serves:** 4

8 to 10 hickory or oak wood chunks

Rub:

2 teaspoons paprika
½ to 1 teaspoon salt
½ teaspoon pepper

3 to 4 pounds beef back ribs (about 8 ribs)

Sauce:

½ cup bottled barbecue sauce
¼ cup frozen orange juice concentrate, thawed
2 tablespoons reduced-sodium soy sauce
1 tablespoon grated fresh ginger

1 At least 1 hour before smoke cooking, soak wood chunks in enough water to cover. Drain before using.

2 For rub, in a small bowl combine paprika, salt, and pepper. Trim fat from ribs. Sprinkle rub evenly over ribs; rub in with your fingers.

3 For sauce, in a small bowl stir together barbecue sauce, orange juice concentrate, soy sauce, and ginger.

4 *In a smoker,* arrange preheated coals, half of the drained wood chunks, and the water pan according to the manufacturer's directions. Pour water into pan. Place ribs, bone side down, on the grill rack over water pan. (Or, place ribs in a rib rack; place on grill rack.) Cover and smoke for 2½ to 3 hours or until ribs are tender, brushing once with sauce during the last 15 minutes of cooking. Add more coals, wood chunks, and water as needed. Pass the remaining sauce with ribs.

Nutrition Facts per serving: 277 cal., 12 g total fat (5 g sat. fat), 79 mg chol., 897 mg sodium, 13 g carbo., 1 g fiber, 28 g pro.
Daily Values: 19% vit. A, 46% vit. C, 3% calcium, 20% iron

keep your smoke sweet

Despite what aficionados may say, there are really only two rules for making great barbecue: Cook low and slow—and keep your smoke sweet. If smoke is stale or acrid, the food will have a strong or bitter taste.

To keep it sweet: 1) Maintain a constant heat source; 2) Keep air flowing through the smoker; and 3) Use seasoned, high-quality wood for smoke. Hickory, oak, cherry, and mesquite all give foods excellent flavor. Avoid any kind of gathered wood from needle-bearing trees such as fir or pine, which have high levels of sap or resin and can make foods bitter.

Texas-Style Beef Ribs

You might figure Texans would be better at cooking beef ribs than anybody in the country. A sweet, chile-infused sauce and mesquite give these meaty ribs a flavor bigger than the Lone Star State itself.

Soak: 1 hour **Prep:** 10 minutes **Smoke:** 1 hour **Serves:** 4

4 cups mesquite or hickory
    wood chips

Sauce:

1 large onion, finely
    chopped
½ cup honey
½ cup catsup
1 4-ounce can diced green
    chile peppers, drained
1 tablespoon chili powder
1 clove garlic, minced
½ teaspoon dry mustard

Rub:

1 teaspoon salt
1 teaspoon black pepper

3 to 4 pounds beef back ribs
    (about 8 ribs)

1 At least 1 hour before smoke cooking, soak wood chips in enough water to cover. Drain before using.

2 For sauce, in a small saucepan stir together onion, honey, catsup, green chile peppers, chili powder, garlic, and mustard. Cook and stir over low heat for 10 minutes.

3 For rub, combine salt and black pepper. Trim fat from ribs. Sprinkle rub evenly over ribs; rub in with your fingers.

4 *In a charcoal grill,* arrange medium-hot coals around a drip pan. Test for medium heat above the pan. Sprinkle half of the drained wood chips over the coals. Place ribs, bone side down, on the grill rack over drip pan. (Or, place ribs in a rib rack; place on grill rack.) Cover and smoke for 1 to 1¼ hours or until ribs are tender, brushing once with sauce during the last 10 minutes of cooking. Add more coals and wood chips as needed. [*In a gas grill,* preheat grill. Reduce heat to medium. Adjust for indirect cooking (see page 6). Add drained wood chips according to the manufacturer's directions. Smoke as above, except place ribs in a roasting pan.] Pass the remaining sauce with ribs.

Nutrition Facts per serving: 403 cal., 12 g total fat (5 g sat. fat), 79 mg chol., 1,125 mg sodium, 49 g carbo., 2 g fiber, 28 g pro.
Daily Values: 20% vit. A, 29% vit. C, 7% calcium, 22% iron

Lamb Roast with Mint SMOKER

A flavorful meat even before it's marinated, rubbed, sauced, or smoked, lamb tastes best with a light smoking. Pecan wood makes for milder smoke flavor than oak.

Prep: 20 minutes **Marinate:** 4 hours **Smoke:** 1¾ hours **Stand:** 10 minutes **Serves:** 6 to 8

Marinade:

- ½ cup mint jelly or ½ cup apple jelly plus 2 tablespoons snipped fresh mint
- ¼ cup white wine vinegar
- 2 tablespoons olive oil or cooking oil
- 1 tablespoon grated onion
- ¼ teaspoon salt
- ¼ teaspoon pepper

- 1 1½- to 2-pound boneless lamb sirloin roast or leg of lamb, rolled and tied
- 6 to 8 pecan or oak wood chunks

1 For marinade, in a small saucepan combine jelly, vinegar, oil, onion, salt, and pepper. Cook and stir over low heat until jelly is melted. Cool.

2 Trim fat from meat. On top side of meat, cut slits about 1½ inches apart and ½ inch deep. Place meat in a plastic bag set in a deep, large bowl. Pour marinade over meat; seal bag. Marinate in refrigerator for 4 to 24 hours, turning bag occasionally.

3 At least 1 hour before smoke cooking, soak wood chunks in enough water to cover. Drain before using. Drain meat, reserving marinade. Insert a meat thermometer into thickest part of meat.

4 *In a smoker,* arrange preheated coals, half of the drained wood chunks, and the water pan according to the manufacturer's directions. Pour water into pan. Place meat on the grill rack over water pan. Cover and smoke until meat thermometer registers 140° for medium-rare (1¾ to 2 hours) or 155° for medium doneness (2¼ to 2½ hours), brushing once with marinade halfway through cooking. Add more coals, wood chunks, and water as needed. Discard the remaining marinade.

5 Remove meat from smoker. Cover meat with foil; let stand for 10 minutes before carving. (The meat's temperature will rise 5° during standing.)

Nutrition Facts per serving: 297 cal., 22 g total fat (9 g sat. fat), 77 mg chol., 73 mg sodium, 5 g carbo., 0 g fiber, 20 g pro.
Daily Values: 1% calcium, 10% iron

Lamb Salad with Roasted Vegetables

This gorgeous salad is perfect for summer entertaining. Arrange spirals of cheese-and-herb-stuffed lamb alongside crisp greens and colorful roasted vegetables.

Soak: 1 hour **Prep:** 15 minutes **Smoke:** 1½ hours **Stand:** 15 minutes **Serves:** 8 to 10

4   cups oak or hickory wood chips
1   3-pound boneless leg of lamb, rolled and tied

Filling:

3   tablespoons grated Parmesan cheese
2   tablespoons snipped fresh parsley
6   cloves garlic, minced
2   teaspoons finely shredded lemon peel

Vegetables:

2   fresh ears of corn, kernels removed, or 2 cups frozen corn, thawed
1   pound tiny new potatoes, quartered
1   small red onion, cut into ½-inch wedges
2   tablespoons olive oil
1   pound asparagus, trimmed and cut into 2-inch pieces, and/or small green beans, trimmed
½   cup bottled vinaigrette salad dressing
¼   cup snipped fresh dill

8   cups torn mixed salad greens
¼   cup Greek ripe olives, pitted and halved

1 At least 1 hour before smoke cooking, soak wood chips in enough water to cover. Drain before using.

2 Unroll meat; trim fat. Sprinkle the meat with salt and pepper. For filling, in a small bowl combine the Parmesan cheese, parsley, garlic, and lemon peel. Spread the filling over meat. Roll up meat; retie securely with 100-percent-cotton string. Insert a meat thermometer into center of meat.

3 *In a charcoal grill*, arrange medium coals around a drip pan. Test for medium-low heat above the pan. Sprinkle half of the drained wood chips over the coals. Place meat on the grill rack over drip pan. Cover and smoke until meat thermometer registers 140° for medium-rare (1½ to 2 hours) or 155° for medium doneness (1¾ to 2¼ hours). Add more coals and wood chips as needed. [*In a gas grill*, preheat grill. Reduce heat to medium-low. Adjust for indirect cooking (see page 6). Add drained wood chips according to the manufacturer's directions. Smoke as above, except place meat on a rack in a roasting pan.]

4 Remove meat. Cover meat with foil; let stand for 15 minutes. (The meat's temperature will rise 5° during standing.)

5 Meanwhile, for vegetables, in a roasting pan toss together the corn, potatoes, and red onion. Drizzle with olive oil; sprinkle with salt and pepper. Roast vegetables in a 425° oven for 15 minutes. Add asparagus and/or green beans; toss to combine. Roast about 15 minutes more or until potatoes are tender. (Serve vegetables warm or at room temperature.)

6 Before serving, toss vegetables with vinaigrette dressing and dill. Arrange salad greens on 8 to 10 dinner plates; top with roasted vegetables. Remove strings from meat; slice meat and arrange next to vegetables. Sprinkle with olives.

Nutrition Facts per serving: 544 cal., 35 g total fat (11 g sat. fat), 114 mg chol., 380 mg sodium, 23 g carbo., 4 g fiber, 37 g pro.
Daily Values: 8% vit. A, 41% vit. C, 7% calcium, 24% iron

Moroccan-Style Lamb Chops SMOKER

These seasoned lamb chops are flavored with a profusion of spices found in abundance at the open-air markets of North Africa. Cool the fire with a creamy yogurt sauce.

Prep: 15 minutes **Marinate:** 6 hours **Smoke:** 55 minutes **Serves:** 4

8 lamb loin chops, cut
   1¼ to 1½ inches thick

Rub:

2 tablespoons sliced green
   onion
1½ teaspoons ground
   coriander
½ teaspoon salt
½ teaspoon ground cumin
½ teaspoon ground
   cardamom
¼ teaspoon ground
   cinnamon
¼ teaspoon ground cloves
¼ teaspoon ground ginger

4 cherry or alder wood
   chunks

Sauce:

1 medium cucumber, seeded
   and chopped (1¼ cups)
1 medium tomato, seeded
   and chopped (½ cup)
½ cup plain low-fat yogurt
⅓ cup chopped onion
⅛ teaspoon salt

   Hot cooked couscous or
   rice (optional)

1 Trim fat from chops. Place chops in a single layer in a shallow dish. For rub, in a small bowl combine green onion, coriander, the ½ teaspoon salt, the cumin, cardamom, cinnamon, cloves, and ginger. Sprinkle mixture evenly over chops; rub in with your fingers. Cover and marinate in the refrigerator for 6 to 24 hours.

2 At least 1 hour before smoke cooking, soak wood chunks in enough water to cover. Drain before using.

3 *In a smoker,* arrange preheated coals, drained wood chunks, and water pan according to the manufacturer's directions. Pour water into pan. Place chops on the grill rack over water pan. Cover and smoke until chops are desired doneness. (Allow 55 to 65 minutes for medium-rare or 65 to 75 minutes for medium doneness.)

4 About 30 minutes before serving, prepare sauce. In a medium bowl combine cucumber, tomato, yogurt, onion, and the ⅛ teaspoon salt. Cover and refrigerate until ready to serve. If desired, serve chops with couscous. Pass the sauce with chops.

Nutrition Facts per serving: 466 cal., 30 g total fat (13 g sat. fat), 142 mg chol., 501 mg sodium, 7 g carbo., 2 g fiber, 40 g pro.
Daily Values: 7% vit. A, 18% vit. C, 11% calcium, 17% iron

Pork

Country Ribs with Peach Sauce

In This Chapter:

Prosciutto-Stuffed Pork ♥ SMOKER

In France, a thin, stuffed-and-rolled piece of meat is called a roulade. In Italy—from where this rustic roast draws its flavor inspiration—it's called a braciola. In any language, it's just plain delicious.

Soak: 1 hour **Prep:** 10 minutes **Smoke:** 1¾ hours **Stand:** 10 minutes **Serves:** 8 to 10

6 to 8 hickory or oak wood chunks

1 2- to 2½-pound boneless pork top loin roast (single loin)

2 tablespoons olive oil

1 to 2 tablespoons snipped fresh rosemary or 1 to 2 teaspoons dried rosemary, crushed

3 ounces thinly sliced prosciutto or dried beef

3 cups spinach leaves, stems removed

2 teaspoons crushed black peppercorns (optional)

1 At least 1 hour before smoke cooking, soak wood chunks in enough water to cover. Drain before using.

2 Trim fat from meat. To butterfly the meat, make a lengthwise cut down the center of the meat, cutting to within ½ inch of the other side, but not through it. Starting at the center of the meat, make one horizontal slit to the right, cutting within ½ inch of the other side. Repeat on the left side of center.

3 Brush the surface of meat with olive oil; sprinkle with rosemary. Cover with the prosciutto, then spinach. Starting from a short side, roll up into a spiral. Tie with 100-percent-cotton string. If desired, brush with additional olive oil and sprinkle with peppercorns. Insert a meat thermometer into the center of meat.

4 *In a smoker,* arrange preheated coals, half of the drained wood chunks, and the water pan according to the manufacturer's directions. Pour water into pan. Place meat on the grill rack over water pan. Cover and smoke for 1¾ to 2 hours or until meat thermometer registers 155°. Add more coals, wood chunks, and water as needed. Remove meat from smoker. Cover meat with foil and let stand for 10 minutes before carving. (The meat's temperature will rise 5° during standing.)

5 To serve, remove strings from meat. Carve meat into ¼- to ½-inch slices, being careful to keep the spiral intact.

Nutrition Facts per serving: 209 cal., 10 g total fat (3 g sat. fat), 69 mg chol., 342 mg sodium, 1 g carbo., 1 g fiber, 28 g pro.
Daily Values: 13% vit. A, 5% vit. C, 3% calcium, 10% iron

Sweetly Spiced Pork Roast ♥

Serving a meat dish this lean means you can splurge a little on the sides. Consider hot buttered spaetzle or noodles, orange-glazed sugar snap peas, and a good German beer.

Soak: 1 hour **Prep:** 10 minutes **Smoke:** 1 hour **Stand:** 10 minutes **Serves:** 8

4 cups apple or alder wood chips

Rub:

¼ cup packed brown sugar
2 cloves garlic, minced
1 teaspoon ground ginger
¼ teaspoon salt
¼ teaspoon pepper
⅛ teaspoon ground cinnamon
   Dash ground cloves

1 2-pound boneless pork top loin roast (single loin)
1 tablespoon soy sauce

1 At least 1 hour before smoke cooking, soak wood chips in enough water to cover. Drain before using.

2 For rub, in a small bowl combine brown sugar, garlic, ginger, salt, pepper, cinnamon, and cloves.

3 Trim fat from meat. Brush soy sauce over surface of meat. Sprinkle rub evenly over meat; rub in with your fingers. Insert a meat thermometer into the center of meat.

4 *In a charcoal grill*, arrange medium coals around a drip pan. Test for medium-low heat above the pan. Sprinkle half of the drained wood chips over the coals. Place meat on the grill rack over drip pan. Cover and smoke for 1 to 1¼ hours or until meat thermometer registers 155°. Add more coals and wood chips as needed. [*In a gas grill*, preheat grill. Reduce heat to medium-low. Adjust for indirect cooking (see page 6). Add drained wood chips according to the manufacturer's directions. Smoke as above, except place meat on a rack in a roasting pan.]

5 Remove meat from grill. Cover meat with foil; let stand for 10 minutes before carving. (The meat's temperature will rise 5° during standing.)

Nutrition Facts per serving: 186 cal., 6 g total fat (2 g sat. fat), 62 mg chol., 231 mg sodium, 7 g carbo., 0 g fiber, 25 g pro.
Daily Values: 1% vit. C, 3% calcium, 6% iron

Smoked Rhubarb-Glazed Pork Roast

When it's rhubarb season, serve this glazed, fruitwood-smoked pork roast with collard or turnip greens, warm corn bread, and (what else?) rhubarb cobbler for dessert.

Soak: 1 hour **Prep:** 10 minutes **Smoke:** 1¼ hours **Stand:** 15 minutes **Serves:** 4 to 6

4 cups apple, cherry, or peach wood chips

Glaze:

12 ounces fresh or frozen rhubarb, sliced (about 2 cups)

1 6-ounce can frozen apple juice concentrate

Few drops red food coloring (optional)

2 tablespoons honey

1 3-pound pork loin center rib roast (backbone loosened)

1 At least 1 hour before smoke cooking, soak wood chips in enough water to cover. Drain before using.

2 For glaze, in a medium saucepan combine rhubarb, apple juice concentrate, and, if desired, red food coloring. Bring to boiling; reduce heat. Cover and simmer for 15 to 20 minutes or until rhubarb is very tender. Strain, pressing liquid out of pulp. Discard pulp. Return liquid to saucepan. Bring to boiling; reduce heat. Simmer, uncovered, about 15 minutes or until rhubarb liquid is reduced to about ½ cup. Remove from heat. Stir in honey.

3 Meanwhile, trim fat from meat. Insert a meat thermometer into center of meat without touching bone.

4 *In a charcoal grill*, arrange medium coals around a drip pan. Test for medium-low heat above the pan. Sprinkle half of the drained wood chips over the coals. Place meat, bone side down, on the grill rack over drip pan. Cover and smoke for 1¼ to 1¾ hours or until meat thermometer registers 155°, brushing once with glaze during the last 15 minutes of cooking. Add more coals and wood chips as needed. [*In a gas grill*, preheat grill. Reduce heat to medium-low. Adjust for indirect cooking (see page 6). Add drained wood chips according to the manufacturer's directions. Smoke as above, except place meat, bone side down, in a roasting pan.] Remove meat from grill.

5 Cover meat with foil; let stand for 15 minutes before carving. (The meat's temperature will rise 5° during standing.) Reheat the remaining glaze and pass with meat.

Nutrition Facts per serving: 391 cal., 15 g total fat (5 g sat. fat), 102 mg chol., 93 mg sodium, 30 g carbo., 2 g fiber, 33 g pro.
Daily Values: 1% vit. A, 13% vit. C, 7% calcium, 12% iron

Coastal Carolina Pulled Pork BBQ

"Pulled" pork simply means that when the meat's done smoking, it's pulled apart into shreds and mixed with sauce before being served on toasted buns and topped with slaw.

Soak: 1 hour **Prep:** 15 minutes **Smoke:** 4 hours **Stand:** 15 minutes **Serves:** 12

8 to 10 oak or hickory wood chunks

Rub:
1½ teaspoons salt
1½ teaspoons black pepper

1 4½- to 5-pound boneless pork shoulder roast

Sauce:
2 cups cider vinegar
3 tablespoons brown sugar (optional)
1 tablespoon salt
1 tablespoon crushed red pepper

12 hamburger buns, split and toasted
Coleslaw (optional)
Bottled hot pepper sauce (optional)

1 At least 1 hour before smoke cooking, soak wood chunks in enough water to cover. Drain before using.

2 For rub, in a small bowl combine the 1½ teaspoons salt and the black pepper. Trim fat from meat. Sprinkle rub evenly over meat; rub in with your fingers. For sauce, in a medium bowl combine vinegar, brown sugar (if desired), the 1 tablespoon salt, and the crushed red pepper. Set aside.

3 *In a smoker,* arrange preheated coals, half of the drained wood chunks, and the water pan according to the manufacturer's directions. Pour water into pan. Place meat on the grill rack over water pan. Cover and smoke for 4 to 5 hours or until meat is very tender. Add more coals, wood chunks, and water as needed.

4 Remove meat from smoker. Cover meat with foil; let stand for 15 minutes. Using 2 forks, gently shred the meat into long, thin strands. Stir in enough of the sauce to moisten the meat.

5 Serve the shredded meat on toasted buns. If desired, top meat with coleslaw. Pass the remaining sauce and, if desired, hot pepper sauce.

Nutrition Facts per serving: 314 cal., 11 g total fat (3 g sat. fat), 64 mg chol., 1,096 mg sodium, 24 g carbo., 1 g fiber, 31 g pro.
Daily Values: 3% vit. A, 1% vit. C, 4% calcium, 17% iron

Maple-Apricot Pork Medallions

You don't want to miss a speck of this sweet and savory sauce. Serve these bacon-wrapped medallions with a toasted almond-studded wild rice pilaf to soak up every drop.

Soak: 1 hour **Prep:** 10 minutes **Smoke:** 20 minutes **Serves:** 6

2 cups maple or oak wood chips
15 slices bacon
2 12-ounce pork tenderloins
Sauce:
1 medium shallot, finely chopped
2 tablespoons butter or margarine
⅔ cup coarsely snipped dried apricots
⅓ cup apricot vinegar, other light-colored fruit-flavored vinegar, or champagne vinegar
2 teaspoons finely shredded orange peel
Dash ground allspice
Dash pepper
¼ cup orange liqueur or orange juice
½ cup maple syrup

1 At least 1 hour before smoke cooking, soak wood chips in enough water to cover. Drain before using.

2 In a large skillet partially cook bacon over medium heat. Drain bacon. Trim fat from meat. Cut meat into 15 slices, each about 1½ inches thick. Wrap a slice of bacon around each meat slice. If desired, secure with a wooden toothpick. Loosely thread the meat onto metal skewers.

3 *In a charcoal grill*, arrange medium-hot coals around a drip pan. Test for medium heat above the pan. Sprinkle the drained wood chips over the coals. Place skewers on the grill rack over drip pan. Cover and smoke for 20 to 22 minutes or until the juices run clear. [*In a gas grill*, preheat grill. Reduce heat to medium. Adjust for indirect cooking (see page 6). Smoke as above, except add drained wood chips according to the manufacturer's directions.]

4 Meanwhile, for sauce, in a medium saucepan cook shallot in butter for 1 minute. Add apricots, vinegar, orange peel, allspice, and pepper. Carefully stir in the orange liqueur. Bring to boiling; reduce heat. Simmer, uncovered, for 8 to 10 minutes or until thickened. Stir in maple syrup; heat through.

5 To serve, remove the meat from skewers and remove any toothpicks. Serve meat with the warm sauce.

Nutrition Facts per serving: 395 cal., 15 g total fat (6 g sat. fat), 97 mg chol., 342 mg sodium, 31 g carbo., 1 g fiber, 29 g pro.
Daily Values: 25% vit. A, 4% vit. C, 4% calcium, 16% iron

Corn Bread-Stuffed Chops

If you'd like to try something other than apple or cherry, maple wood would also give these hearty chops a smoky-sweet flavor. Serve them with sweet corn, steamed carrots, and hot biscuits.

Soak: 1 hour **Prep:** 10 minutes **Smoke:** 35 minutes **Serves:** 4

2 cups apple or cherry wood chips

Rub:
- ¼ teaspoon black pepper
- ⅛ teaspoon celery seed
- ⅛ teaspoon onion salt
- Dash ground cloves
- Dash ground red pepper (optional)

Stuffing:
- 4 ounces bulk pork sausage or bulk turkey sausage
- ¼ cup chopped onion
- ½ cup corn bread stuffing mix
- ¼ cup dried cranberries
- ½ of a 4-ounce can diced green chile peppers, drained
- 2 tablespoons snipped fresh parsley
- 1 to 2 tablespoons apple juice or water

4 pork loin rib chops, cut 1½ inches thick

1 At least 1 hour before smoke cooking, soak wood chips in enough water to cover. Drain before using.

2 For rub, in a small bowl combine black pepper, celery seed, onion salt, cloves, and, if desired, ground red pepper. Set aside.

3 For stuffing, in a small saucepan cook the sausage and onion until sausage is brown and onion is tender. Drain well. Stir in the stuffing mix, cranberries, green chile peppers, and parsley. Toss with enough apple juice just to moisten.

4 Trim fat from chops. Make a pocket in each chop by cutting horizontally from the fat side almost to the bone. Spoon stuffing into pockets. If necessary, secure openings with wooden toothpicks. Sprinkle rub evenly over chops; rub in with your fingers.

5 *In a charcoal grill,* arrange medium-hot coals around a drip pan. Test for medium heat above the pan. Sprinkle the drained wood chips over the coals. Place chops on the grill rack over drip pan. Cover and smoke for 35 to 40 minutes or until the juices run clear. [*In a gas grill,* preheat grill. Reduce heat to medium. Adjust for indirect cooking (see page 6). Smoke as above, except add drained wood chips according to the manufacturer's directions.] Remove any toothpicks before serving.

Nutrition Facts per serving: 425 cal., 13 g total fat (4 g sat. fat), 146 mg chol., 470 mg sodium, 17 g carbo., 1 g fiber, 55 g pro.
Daily Values: 2% vit. A, 15% vit. C, 6% calcium, 16% iron

Chops with Cherry Salsa SMOKER

Some folks just crave the taste sensation of sweet and hot. In this refreshing salsa, the sweet comes from dried cherries, the heat from chili sauce.

Soak: 1 hour **Prep:** 5 minutes **Smoke:** 1¾ hours **Serves:** 4

6 to 8 cherry, orange, or
    apple wood chunks
Salsa:
  ½ cup dried tart or sweet
    cherries, snipped
  ½ cup bottled chili sauce
  ½ teaspoon finely shredded
    orange peel
  ¼ cup orange juice
  2 tablespoons thinly sliced
    green onion

  4 pork loin chops, cut
    1½ inches thick

1 At least 1 hour before smoke cooking, soak wood chunks in enough water to cover. Drain before using.

2 For salsa, in a small saucepan combine the cherries, chili sauce, orange peel, orange juice, and green onion. Bring just to boiling; remove from heat. Cool to room temperature.

3 Trim fat from chops. Sprinkle both sides of the chops with salt and pepper.

4 *In a smoker*, arrange preheated coals, half of the drained wood chunks, and the water pan according to the manufacturer's directions. Pour water into pan. Place chops on the grill rack over water pan. Cover and smoke for 1¾ to 2¼ hours or until the juices run clear. Add more coals, wood chunks, and water as needed. Serve the chops with salsa.

Nutrition Facts per serving: 407 cal., 12 g total fat (4 g sat. fat), 133 mg chol., 497 mg sodium, 21 g carbo., 3 g fiber, 50 g pro.
Daily Values: 5% vit. A, 24% vit. C, 5% calcium, 12% iron

what sort of wood

When smoke cooking, use only hardwoods such as oak, hickory, pecan, or maple; or fruitwoods such as apple, cherry, orange, or peach. Avoid using gathered wood from softwood trees such as pine or fir. Their high levels of resin or sap will give foods a harsh taste.

Some smoke flavors complement certain foods better than others. In general, mesquite is great with beef, though hickory and oak are nice, too. Hickory, apple, and pecan are perfect with pork. Orange and hickory are naturals with chicken and turkey. And most salmon smokers wouldn't think of using anything other than alder or apple wood.

Caribbean Smoked Chops SMOKER

Look for a mango that has smooth, unblemished skin and flesh that yields to gentle pressure. If the mango is too firm, ripen it in a paper bag at room temperature for a few days.

Soak: 1 hour **Prep:** 10 minutes **Smoke:** 1¾ hours **Serves:** 4

6 to 8 pecan or cherry wood chunks

4 pork loin chops, cut 1½ inches thick

2 to 3 teaspoons Jamaican jerk seasoning

Sauce:

1 medium mango, peeled, seeded, and finely chopped (about 1 cup)

2 green onions, sliced

2 tablespoons snipped fresh parsley or snipped fresh cilantro

½ teaspoon finely shredded orange peel

2 teaspoons orange juice

¼ teaspoon Jamaican jerk seasoning

Fresh cilantro sprigs (optional)

1 At least 1 hour before smoke cooking, soak the wood chunks in enough water to cover. Drain before using.

2 Trim fat from chops. Sprinkle the 2 to 3 teaspoons jerk seasoning evenly over chops; rub in with your fingers.

3 *In a smoker,* arrange preheated coals, half of the drained wood chunks, and the water pan according to the manufacturer's directions. Pour water into pan. Place chops on the grill rack over water pan. Cover and smoke for 1¾ to 2¼ hours or until the juices run clear. Add more coals, wood chunks, and water as needed.

4 Meanwhile, for sauce, in a medium bowl stir together mango, green onions, parsley, orange peel, orange juice, and the ¼ teaspoon jerk seasoning. Let stand at room temperature for 15 to 20 minutes to blend flavors. Serve the sauce over chops. If desired, garnish with cilantro sprigs.

Nutrition Facts per serving: 357 cal., 11 g total fat (4 g sat. fat), 124 mg chol., 188 mg sodium, 11 g carbo., 1 g fiber, 50 g pro.
Daily Values: 43% vit. A, 35% vit. C, 7% calcium, 13% iron

Orange and Rosemary Chops

Molasses comes in three strengths: Light molasses is mildest in flavor, blackstrap is very strong, and dark is somewhere in the middle. For more molasses flavor, use the dark or blackstrap variety in this recipe.

Prep: 15 minutes **Marinate:** 4 hours **Smoke:** 35 minutes **Serves:** 4

4 boneless pork loin chops,
   cut 1½ inches thick
Marinade:
2 teaspoons finely shredded
   orange peel
½ cup orange juice
2 tablespoons olive oil
2 tablespoons white wine
   Worcestershire sauce
1 tablespoon snipped fresh
   rosemary or 1 teaspoon
   dried rosemary, crushed
1 tablespoon molasses
2 teaspoons sugar
¼ teaspoon salt
⅛ teaspoon pepper

2 cups orange, apple, or
   peach wood chips

1 Trim fat from chops. Place chops in a plastic bag set in a shallow dish. For marinade, in a small bowl combine orange peel, orange juice, olive oil, Worcestershire sauce, rosemary, molasses, sugar, salt, and pepper.

2 Pour marinade over chops; seal bag. Marinate in the refrigerator for 4 to 24 hours, turning bag occasionally.

3 At least 1 hour before smoke cooking, soak wood chips in enough water to cover. Drain before using. Drain chops, reserving marinade.

4 *In a charcoal grill*, arrange medium-hot coals around a drip pan. Test for medium heat above the pan. Sprinkle the drained wood chips over the coals. Place chops on the grill rack over drip pan. Cover and smoke for 35 to 40 minutes or until the juices run clear, brushing once with marinade halfway through cooking. [*In a gas grill*, preheat grill. Reduce heat to medium. Adjust for indirect cooking (see page 6). Smoke as above, except add drained wood chips according to the manufacturer's directions.] Discard the remaining marinade.

Nutrition Facts per serving: 364 cal., 14 g total fat (4 g sat. fat), 124 mg chol., 187 mg sodium, 5 g carbo., 0 g fiber, 50 g pro.
Daily Values: 1% vit. A, 15% vit. C, 6% calcium, 11% iron

Maple-Barbecue Glazed Chops ♥

If you're sweet on the flavor of maple, these succulent chops will please your taste buds. They get a double dose of the stuff—in a quick-to-fix glaze and a slow smoking over maple wood.

Soak: 1 hour **Prep:** 10 minutes **Smoke:** 35 minutes **Serves:** 4

2 cups maple or oak wood chips

Glaze:
¾ cup maple syrup
2 tablespoons bottled chili sauce
2 tablespoons cider vinegar
1 tablespoon finely chopped onion
1 tablespoon Worcestershire sauce
½ teaspoon salt
½ teaspoon dry mustard
½ teaspoon pepper

4 bone-in or boneless pork loin chops, cut 1¼ inches thick

1 At least 1 hour before smoke cooking, soak wood chips in enough water to cover. Drain before using.

2 For glaze, in a small saucepan combine maple syrup, chili sauce, vinegar, onion, Worcestershire sauce, salt, dry mustard, and pepper. Bring to boiling; reduce heat. Simmer, uncovered, about 5 minutes or until slightly thickened. Remove from heat. Trim fat from chops.

3 *In a charcoal grill*, arrange medium-hot coals around a drip pan. Test for medium heat above the pan. Sprinkle the drained wood chips over the coals. Place chops on the grill rack over drip pan. Cover and smoke for 35 to 40 minutes or until the juices run clear, brushing once with glaze during the last 10 minutes of cooking. [*In a gas grill*, preheat grill. Reduce heat to medium. Adjust for indirect cooking (see page 6). Smoke as above, except add drained wood chips according to the manufacturer's directions.] Reheat the remaining glaze and pass with chops.

Nutrition Facts per serving: 446 cal., 10 g total fat (3 g sat. fat), 108 mg chol., 510 mg sodium, 44 g carbo., 1 g fiber, 44 g pro.
Daily Values: 1% vit. A, 4% vit. C, 9% calcium, 15% iron

barbecue companions

The savory concoctions known as rubs, marinades, and mops add great flavor to smoked foods. **Rubs** are a combination of spices—dry or wet—that are rubbed into the surface of the meat before it's cooked. Rubs form a tasty crust and seal in the flavor of the meat. **Marinades** are flavorful liquid mixtures that foods soak in before they're cooked. **Mops** are applied to the meat during cooking. Mops do two things: create a flavorful "bark" and seal in moisture. They might contain vinegar, meat broth, fruit juice, water, seasonings, butter, or oils. Mops are usually applied with a cotton-string tool that looks like a miniature floor mop.

Mustard-Bourbon Glazed Ribs SMOKER

Kentuckians are proud of their bourbon (named for Bourbon County, Kentucky) and their barbecue. Here the two join forces in a classic messy-but-worth-it rib extravaganza.

Prep: 15 minutes **Marinate:** 1 hour **Smoke:** 3 hours **Serves:** 4

Rub:
- 1½ teaspoons pepper
- ¾ teaspoon paprika
- ½ teaspoon garlic salt or onion salt

- 3 to 3½ pounds pork country-style ribs
- 8 to 10 oak or hickory wood chunks

Sauce:
- ¼ cup brown mustard
- ¼ cup bourbon or orange juice
- ¼ cup molasses
- 2 tablespoons brown sugar
- 2 tablespoons soy sauce
- 1 teaspoon cooking oil

1 For rub, in a small bowl stir together the pepper, paprika, and garlic salt. Trim fat from ribs. Place ribs in a shallow dish. Sprinkle the rub evenly over ribs; rub in with your fingers. Cover and marinate in the refrigerator for 1 to 4 hours.

2 At least 1 hour before smoke cooking, soak wood chunks in enough water to cover. Drain before using.

3 *In a smoker*, arrange preheated coals, half of the drained wood chunks, and the water pan according to the manufacturer's directions. Pour water into pan. Place ribs, bone side down, on the grill rack over water pan. (Or, place ribs in a rib rack; place on grill rack.) Cover and smoke for 3 to 4 hours or until ribs are tender. Add more coals, wood chunks, and water as needed.

4 Meanwhile, for sauce, in a small saucepan combine the mustard, bourbon, molasses, brown sugar, soy sauce, and cooking oil. Cook and stir over low heat until heated through.

5 Before serving, brush ribs with some of the sauce. Pass the remaining sauce.

Nutrition Facts per serving: 497 cal., 24 g total fat (8 g sat. fat), 135 mg chol., 899 mg sodium, 20 g carbo., 0 g fiber, 41 g pro.
Daily Values: 5% vit. A, 2% vit. C, 11% calcium, 19% iron

Chinese Smoked Ribs

Amid all the stir-fries and egg rolls, it's easy to forget the Chinese have spent centuries mastering the art of barbecue. These pork ribs enjoy the benefits of a dry rub and a ginger-infused sauce.

Prep: 15 minutes **Marinate:** 6 hours **Smoke:** 1¼ hours **Serves:** 6

Rub:
- 2 tablespoons granulated sugar
- ½ teaspoon salt
- ¼ teaspoon paprika
- ¼ teaspoon ground turmeric
- ¼ teaspoon celery seed
- ¼ teaspoon dry mustard

- 4 pounds pork loin back ribs or meaty spareribs

Sauce:
- ¼ cup catsup
- ¼ cup soy sauce
- 2 tablespoons brown sugar
- 2 tablespoons water
- 1 teaspoon grated fresh ginger or 1 teaspoon ground ginger

- 4 cups alder or oak wood chips

1 For rub, in a small bowl combine granulated sugar, salt, paprika, turmeric, celery seed, and dry mustard. Trim fat from ribs. Place ribs in a shallow dish. Sprinkle the rub evenly over ribs; rub in with your fingers. Cover and marinate in the refrigerator for 6 to 24 hours.

2 For sauce, in a small bowl combine catsup, soy sauce, brown sugar, water, and ginger. Cover and refrigerate for 6 to 24 hours.

3 At least 1 hour before smoke cooking, soak wood chips in enough water to cover. Drain before using.

4 *In a charcoal grill,* arrange medium-hot coals around a drip pan. Test for medium heat above the pan. Sprinkle half of the drained wood chips over the coals. Place ribs, bone side down, on the grill rack over drip pan. (Or, place ribs in a rib rack; place on grill rack.) Cover and smoke for 1¼ to 1½ hours or until ribs are tender, brushing once with sauce during the last 15 minutes of cooking. Add more coals and wood chips as needed. [*In a gas grill,* preheat grill. Reduce heat to medium. Adjust for indirect cooking (see page 6). Add drained wood chips according to the manufacturer's directions. Smoke as above, except place ribs in a roasting pan.] Before serving, brush ribs with the remaining sauce.

Nutrition Facts per serving: 377 cal., 17 g total fat (6 g sat. fat), 84 mg chol., 1,061 mg sodium, 12 g carbo., 0 g fiber, 41 g pro.
Daily Values: 2% vit. A, 3% vit. C, 2% calcium, 13% iron

Country Ribs with Peach Sauce

Country food is known to be laid-back, lip-smacking, and generously proportioned. Country-style ribs are no exception. These meaty, peach-glazed ribs are just right for hearty appetites.

Soak: 1 hour **Prep:** 10 minutes **Smoke:** 1½ hours **Serves:** 4

4 cups peach, apple, or alder
    wood chips
Sauce:
1 15- to 16-ounce can peach
    slices, drained
1 medium onion, chopped
¼ cup light-colored corn
    syrup or honey
2 tablespoons steak sauce
¼ teaspoon ground cumin
½ cup peach chutney
1 or 2 fresh jalapeño
    peppers, seeded and
    finely chopped

2½ to 3 pounds pork country-
    style ribs

1 At least 1 hour before smoke cooking, soak wood chips in enough water to cover. Drain before using.

2 For sauce, in a blender container or food processor bowl combine the peach slices, onion, corn syrup, steak sauce, and cumin. Cover and blend or process until nearly smooth. Pour into a small saucepan. Stir in the chutney and jalapeño peppers. Cook and stir over low heat until heated through. Trim fat from ribs.

3 *In a charcoal grill*, arrange medium-hot coals around a drip pan. Test for medium heat above the pan. Sprinkle half of the drained wood chips over the coals. Place ribs, bone side down, on the grill rack over drip pan. (Or, place ribs in a rib rack; place on grill rack.) Cover and smoke for 1½ to 2 hours or until ribs are tender, brushing once with sauce during the last 15 minutes of cooking. Add more coals and wood chips as needed. [*In a gas grill*, preheat grill. Reduce heat to medium. Adjust for indirect cooking (see page 6). Add drained wood chips according to the manufacturer's directions. Smoke as above, except place ribs in a roasting pan.]

4 Reheat the remaining sauce and pass with ribs. If desired, garnish ribs with additional jalapeño peppers.

Nutrition Facts per serving: 469 cal., 15 g total fat (5 g sat. fat), 69 mg chol., 230 mg sodium, 67 g carbo., 2 g fiber, 19 g pro.
Daily Values: 33% vit. A, 34% vit. C, 2% calcium, 6% iron

Spicy Hoisin-Honey Ribs SMOKER

Hoisin's other name—Peking sauce—hints at its use in China's famous duck dish. Thick and reddish-brown in color, hoisin sauce is a sweet and spicy medley of soybeans, garlic, chile peppers, and spices.

Prep: 15 minutes **Marinate:** 1 hour **Smoke:** 3 hours **Serves:** 4

Rub:
- 1 tablespoon paprika
- ½ teaspoon coarsely ground black pepper
- ¼ teaspoon onion salt

- 4 pounds pork loin back ribs
- 1 lime, halved
- 8 to 10 oak or hickory wood chunks

Sauce:
- 1 to 2 tablespoons finely chopped canned chipotle peppers in adobo sauce or 2 dried chipotle peppers
- ½ cup bottled hoisin sauce
- ¼ cup honey
- 2 tablespoons cider vinegar
- 2 tablespoons Dijon-style mustard
- 2 cloves garlic, minced

1 For rub, in a small bowl combine paprika, black pepper, and onion salt. Trim fat from ribs. Place ribs in a shallow dish. Squeeze and rub the cut surfaces of the lime halves over ribs. Sprinkle the rub evenly over ribs; rub in with your fingers. Cover and marinate in the refrigerator for 1 to 4 hours.

2 At least 1 hour before smoke cooking, soak wood chunks in enough water to cover. Drain before using.

3 *In a smoker*, arrange preheated coals, half of the drained wood chunks, and the water pan according to the manufacturer's directions. Pour water into pan. Place ribs, bone side down, on the grill rack over water pan. (Or, place ribs in a rib rack; place on grill rack.) Cover and smoke for 3 to 4 hours or until ribs are tender. Add more coals, wood chunks, and water as needed.

4 Meanwhile, for sauce, if using dried chipotle peppers, soak them in warm water for 30 minutes; drain well and finely chop. In a small saucepan stir together the chipotle peppers in sauce or dried peppers, hoisin sauce, honey, vinegar, mustard, and garlic. Cook and stir over low heat until heated through.

5 Before serving, brush ribs with some of the sauce. Pass the remaining sauce.

Nutrition Facts per serving: 509 cal., 25 g total fat (8 g sat. fat), 110 mg chol., 898 mg sodium, 40 g carbo., 1 g fiber, 28 g pro.
Daily Values: 19% vit. A, 8% vit. C, 4% calcium, 11% iron

Sugar-Smoked Pork Ribs SMOKER

These ribs are the essence of simplicity but still manage to cover nearly all the flavor bases for perfect balance: brown sugar for sweetness; fresh lemon for sour; and a little soy for salty.

Soak: 1 hour **Prep:** 15 minutes **Smoke:** 3 hours **Serves:** 6

8 to 10 apple or hickory
    wood chunks
4 pounds meaty pork
    spareribs
1 lemon, halved
1 to 2 tablespoons soy sauce
¼ cup packed brown sugar

1 At least 1 hour before smoke cooking, soak wood chunks in enough water to cover. Drain before using.

2 Trim fat from ribs. Place ribs in a shallow dish. Squeeze and rub the cut surfaces of the lemon halves over ribs. Brush ribs with soy sauce. Cover and marinate in the refrigerator for 1 hour.

3 *In a smoker,* arrange preheated coals, half of the drained wood chunks, and the water pan according to the manufacturer's directions. Pour water into pan. Place ribs, bone side down, on the grill rack over water pan. (Or, place ribs in a rib rack; place on grill rack.) Cover and smoke for 3 to 4 hours or until ribs are tender. Add more coals, wood chunks, and water as needed.

4 Sprinkle the ribs with brown sugar. Cover and smoke for 5 minutes more.

Nutrition Facts per serving: 548 cal., 39 g total fat (14 g sat. fat), 156 mg chol., 276 mg sodium, 10 g carbo., 0 g fiber, 38 g pro.
Daily Values: 6% vit. C, 7% calcium, 14% iron

the weather affect

The ideal weather conditions for smoke cooking are 60° and above on a still, windless day—in other words, the perfect fall day. You can certainly smoke-cook on a cold and/or windy day, but you may need to allow for a longer cooking time than is specified in the recipe.

Bratwurst with Onions

Some things were just meant for each other: milk and cookies, tea and crumpets, beer and brats. A stronger-tasting beer for the marinade—such as a stout or a porter—will give the links more flavor.

Prep: 15 minutes **Marinate:** 6 hours **Smoke:** 20 minutes **Serves:** 8

8 uncooked bratwurst links
Marinade:
1 12-ounce can beer
2 tablespoons brown sugar
1 tablespoon prepared
  mustard
1 teaspoon chili powder
  Several dashes bottled hot
  pepper sauce

2 cups hickory or oak wood
  chips
3 medium onions, sliced
3 tablespoons margarine or
  butter
1 teaspoon chili powder
8 French-style rolls, split and
  toasted

1 Use the tines of a fork to prick several holes in each bratwurst. Place bratwurst in a plastic bag set in a shallow dish. For marinade, in a medium bowl combine beer, brown sugar, mustard, 1 teaspoon chili powder, and the hot pepper sauce. Pour over bratwurst; seal bag. Marinate in the refrigerator for 6 to 24 hours, turning bag occasionally.

2 At least 1 hour before smoke cooking, soak wood chips in enough water to cover. Drain before using.

3 Fold a 36×18-inch piece of heavy foil in half to make an 18-inch square. Place onions in center of foil. Dot with margarine and sprinkle with 1 teaspoon chili powder. Bring up 2 opposite edges of foil and seal with a double fold. Fold remaining ends to completely enclose onions, leaving space for steam to build. Refrigerate the packet until ready to cook. Drain bratwurst, reserving marinade.

4 *In a charcoal grill*, arrange medium-hot coals around a drip pan. Test for medium heat above the pan. Sprinkle the drained wood chips over the coals. Place bratwurst on the grill rack over drip pan. Cover and smoke for 20 to 25 minutes or until bratwurst juices run clear, brushing once with marinade halfway through cooking. Place onion packet next to bratwurst on grill rack directly over coals during the last 10 to 15 minutes of cooking. [*In a gas grill*, preheat grill. Reduce heat to medium. Adjust for indirect cooking (see page 6). Smoke as above, except add drained wood chips according to the manufacturer's directions.] Discard the remaining marinade.

5 Remove bratwurst and packet from grill. Serve bratwurst on toasted rolls and top with onions.

Nutrition Facts per serving: 451 cal., 32 g total fat (10 g sat. fat), 51 mg chol., 908 mg sodium, 25 g carbo., 2 g fiber, 14 g pro.
Daily Values: 7% vit. A, 5% vit. C, 8% calcium, 13% iron

Poultry

Double-Glazed Turkey Breasts

In This Chapter:

Smoked Gremolata Chicken SMOKER

Gremolata—the garnish of garlic, lemon, and parsley that's traditionally sprinkled over the Italian dish called osso buco (braised veal shanks)—gives this smoked bird great flavor.

Soak: 1 hour **Prep:** 15 minutes **Smoke:** 3¼ hours **Stand:** 15 minutes **Serves:** 6 to 8

8 to 10 apple or cherry wood chunks

Rub:

2 to 3 tablespoons snipped fresh Italian flat-leaf parsley

2 teaspoons finely shredded lemon peel

¼ teaspoon coarsely ground pepper

1 6- to 7-pound whole roasting chicken

1 garlic bulb

1 small lemon, cut into wedges
Fresh Italian flat-leaf parsley sprigs

1 At least 1 hour before smoke cooking, soak wood chunks in enough water to cover. Drain before using.

2 For rub, in a small bowl combine the snipped parsley, the lemon peel, and pepper. Remove the neck and giblets from chicken. Sprinkle rub evenly over chicken; rub in with your fingers.

3 With a sharp knife, cut off the top ½ inch from garlic bulb to expose the ends of the individual cloves. Leaving garlic bulb whole, remove any loose, papery outer layers. Place the garlic bulb and lemon wedges in cavity of chicken. Skewer the neck skin to the back. Twist wing tips under back. Tie legs to tail with 100-percent-cotton string. Insert a meat thermometer into the center of an inside thigh muscle without touching bone.

4 *In a smoker,* arrange preheated coals, half of the drained wood chunks, and the water pan according to the manufacturer's directions. Pour water into pan. Place chicken, breast side up, on the grill rack over water pan. Cover and smoke for 3¼ to 4 hours or until meat thermometer registers 180°. Add more coals, wood chunks, and water as needed. Remove chicken from smoker. Cover chicken with foil; let stand for 15 minutes before carving.

5 Remove garlic and lemon wedges from chicken cavity. If desired, season chicken with salt. Garnish with parsley sprigs and additional lemon wedges.

Nutrition Facts per serving: 363 cal., 20 g total fat (6 g sat. fat), 162 mg chol., 120 mg sodium, 2 g carbo., 0 g fiber, 41 g pro.
Daily Values: 29% vit. A, 8% vit. C, 2% calcium, 17% iron

Italian Marinated Chicken

Crushing dried herbs releases natural oils so their flavor and aroma are as potent as they can be when used in cooking. To crush them, simply rub them between your fingers.

Prep: 10 minutes **Marinate:** 8 hours **Smoke:** 50 minutes **Serves:** 4 to 6

4 to 6 medium chicken breast halves (2 to 3 pounds total)

Marinade:
1½ cups dry white wine
½ cup olive oil
1 tablespoon dried Italian seasoning, crushed
4 cloves garlic, minced

2 cups alder or apple wood chips

1 If desired, remove skin from the chicken. Place chicken in a plastic bag set in a shallow dish.

2 For marinade, in a medium bowl stir together the wine, olive oil, Italian seasoning, and garlic. Pour over chicken; seal bag. Marinate in the refrigerator for at least 8 hours or overnight, turning bag occasionally.

3 At least 1 hour before smoke cooking, soak wood chips in enough water to cover. Drain before using. Drain chicken, reserving marinade.

4 *In a charcoal grill*, arrange medium-hot coals around a drip pan. Test for medium heat above the pan. Sprinkle the drained wood chips over the coals. Place chicken, bone side down, on the grill rack over drip pan. Cover and smoke for 50 to 60 minutes or until chicken is tender and juices run clear, brushing once with marinade halfway through cooking. [*In a gas grill*, preheat grill. Reduce heat to medium. Adjust for indirect cooking (see page 6). Smoke as above, except add drained wood chips according to the manufacturer's directions.] Discard the remaining marinade.

Nutrition Facts per serving: 302 cal., 19 g total fat (5 g sat. fat), 94 mg chol., 75 mg sodium, 0 g carbo., 0 g fiber, 29 g pro.
Daily Values: 2% vit. A, 2% vit. C, 2% calcium, 6% iron

Orange-Dijon Chicken

A jar of Dijon mustard is a staple in every good cook's pantry. In this flavorful sauce, its pungence is tamed by the sweetness of orange juice, balsamic vinegar, and fresh herbs.

Prep: 10 minutes **Marinate:** 4 hours **Smoke:** 15 minutes **Serves:** 4

4 medium skinless, boneless chicken breast halves (about 1 pound total)

Marinade:
½ cup olive oil
3 cloves garlic, minced
½ teaspoon salt
⅛ teaspoon pepper

2 cups orange or apple wood chips
1 recipe Orange-Dijon Sauce
Coarsely ground pepper

1 Place chicken in a plastic bag set in a shallow dish. For marinade, in a small bowl combine the olive oil, garlic, salt, and the ⅛ teaspoon pepper. Pour over chicken; seal bag. Marinate in the refrigerator for 4 to 8 hours, turning bag occasionally.

2 At least 1 hour before smoke cooking, soak wood chips in enough water to cover. Drain before using. Prepare Orange-Dijon Sauce. Cover and refrigerate until ready to serve. Drain chicken, discarding marinade.

3 *In a charcoal grill*, arrange medium-hot coals around a drip pan. Test for medium heat above the pan. Sprinkle the drained wood chips over the coals. Place chicken on the grill rack over drip pan. Cover and smoke for 15 to 18 minutes or until chicken is tender and juices run clear. [*In a gas grill*, preheat grill. Reduce heat to medium. Adjust for indirect cooking (see page 6). Smoke as above, except add drained wood chips according to the manufacturer's directions.]

4 Meanwhile, in a small saucepan cook and stir sauce over medium-low heat until heated through. Transfer the chicken to 4 dinner plates and, if desired, cut into slices. Spoon the sauce over chicken and sprinkle with the coarsely ground pepper.

Orange-Dijon Sauce: In a small bowl combine ¼ cup frozen orange juice concentrate, thawed; 2 to 4 tablespoons Dijon-style mustard; 2 tablespoons water; 1 tablespoon balsamic vinegar (if desired); 1 tablespoon olive oil; 1 teaspoon snipped fresh basil; 1 teaspoon snipped fresh mint; and ½ teaspoon snipped fresh rosemary. Makes about ¾ cup.

Nutrition Facts per serving: 266 cal., 13 g total fat (2 g sat. fat), 66 mg chol., 221 mg sodium, 9 g carbo., 0 g fiber, 28 g pro.
Daily Values: 2% vit. A, 44% vit. C, 4% calcium, 7% iron

Peanut-Ginger Chicken

Peanut sauce is popular the world over—in Asia, Africa, Mexico, and South America. This sweet and spicy dish takes a few cues from each of those places, with delicious results.

Prep: 15 minutes **Marinate:** 12 hours **Smoke:** 50 minutes **Serves:** 6

12 chicken thighs (about 3 pounds total)

Marinade:
- ½ cup water
- ½ cup creamy peanut butter
- ¼ cup bottled chili sauce
- ¼ cup soy sauce
- 2 tablespoons cooking oil
- 2 tablespoons vinegar
- 1 tablespoon grated fresh ginger or ¾ teaspoon ground ginger
- 4 cloves garlic, minced
- ¼ to ½ teaspoon ground red pepper

Salsa:
- 1 cup chopped fresh fruit (such as peeled peaches, nectarines, mangoes, pears, and/or plums)
- 1 cup chopped, seeded cucumber
- 2 tablespoons thinly sliced green onion
- 2 tablespoons snipped fresh parsley or cilantro
- 1 tablespoon sugar
- 1 tablespoon cooking oil
- 1 tablespoon vinegar

2 cups hickory, pecan, or oak wood chips

1 If desired, remove skin from chicken. Place chicken in a plastic bag set in a shallow dish.

2 For marinade, in a medium bowl gradually stir water into peanut butter. (The mixture will stiffen at first.) Stir in the chili sauce, soy sauce, the 2 tablespoons oil, the 2 tablespoons vinegar, the ginger, garlic, and ground red pepper. Pour over chicken; seal bag. Marinate in the refrigerator for 12 to 24 hours, turning bag occasionally.

3 For salsa, in another medium bowl combine the fruit, cucumber, green onion, parsley, sugar, the 1 tablespoon oil, and the 1 tablespoon vinegar. Cover and refrigerate for 1 to 2 hours to blend flavors.

4 At least 1 hour before smoke cooking, soak wood chips in enough water to cover. Drain before using. Drain chicken, reserving marinade.

5 *In a charcoal grill*, arrange medium-hot coals around a drip pan. Test for medium heat above the pan. Sprinkle the drained wood chips over the coals. Place chicken on the grill rack over drip pan. Cover and smoke for 50 to 60 minutes or until chicken is tender and juices run clear, brushing once with marinade halfway through cooking. [*In a gas grill*, preheat grill. Reduce heat to medium. Adjust for indirect cooking (see page 6). Smoke as above, except add drained wood chips according to the manufacturer's directions.] Discard the remaining marinade. Spoon some of the salsa over chicken; pass the remaining salsa.

Nutrition Facts per serving: 420 cal., 29 g total fat (7 g sat. fat), 110 mg chol., 506 mg sodium, 13 g carbo., 2 g fiber, 27 g pro.
Daily Values: 12% vit. A, 17% vit. C, 3% calcium, 9% iron

Smokin' Jerk Chicken SMOKER

Smoke is a main flavoring agent in authentic Jamaican jerk—pork or chicken that's spiced with thyme, allspice, and Scotch Bonnet peppers before it's slow-cooked over the wood of the allspice tree.

Prep: 15 minutes **Marinate:** 1 hour **Smoke:** 1½ hours **Serves:** 6

3 pounds meaty chicken
   pieces (breasts, thighs,
   and drumsticks)

Marinade:
½ cup tomato juice
⅓ cup finely chopped onion
2 tablespoons water
2 tablespoons lime juice
1 tablespoon cooking oil
1 tablespoon Pickapeppa
   sauce (optional)
4 cloves garlic, minced
½ teaspoon salt

6 to 8 fruitwood chunks
1 to 2 tablespoons Jamaican
   jerk seasoning
   Lime wedges

1 If desired, remove skin from chicken. Place chicken in a plastic bag set in a shallow dish. For marinade, in a small bowl combine tomato juice, onion, water, lime juice, oil, Pickapeppa sauce (if desired), garlic, and salt. Pour over chicken; seal bag. Marinate in the refrigerator for 1 to 4 hours, turning bag occasionally.

2 At least 1 hour before smoke cooking, soak wood chunks in enough water to cover. Drain before using. Drain chicken, discarding marinade. Sprinkle jerk seasoning evenly over chicken; rub in with your fingers.

3 *In a smoker*, arrange preheated coals, half of the drained wood chunks, and the water pan according to the manufacturer's directions. Pour water into pan. Place chicken on the grill rack over water pan. Cover and smoke for 1½ to 2 hours or until chicken is tender and juices run clear. Add more coals, wood chunks, and water as needed. Serve chicken with lime wedges.

Nutrition Facts per serving: 283 cal., 14 g total fat (4 g sat. fat), 104 mg chol., 331 mg sodium, 3 g carbo., 0 g fiber, 34 g pro.
Daily Values: 2% vit. A, 8% vit. C, 3% calcium, 10% iron

make mine marinated

A good soak is good for the soul—and it's good for your food, too. Marinating does two great things: It adds flavor and it tenderizes meats. The best way to marinate is in a large self-sealing plastic bag set in a shallow dish in the refrigerator. Turn the bag every few hours to distribute the marinade equally. For safety's sake, avoid brushing food with marinades that may contain raw meat juices during the last half of cooking. Keep marinades you are planning to brush on meats, poultry, or fish halfway through the cooking time in the refrigerator, and be sure to thoroughly wash your basting brush with hot soapy water after use.

Sweet 'n' Sticky Chicken SMOKER

Tie a napkin around your neck and dig into this American barbecue classic. Serve it with a garden vegetable salad, whole wheat rolls, and fresh berries for dessert.

Soak: 1 hour **Prep:** 5 minutes **Smoke:** 1½ hours **Serves:** 6

6 to 8 maple or hickory
    wood chunks

6 whole chicken legs
    (drumstick and thigh)

Rub:

1½ teaspoons dried oregano,
    crushed

1½ teaspoons dried thyme,
    crushed

½ teaspoon garlic salt

¼ teaspoon onion powder

¼ teaspoon pepper

1 recipe Sweet 'n' Sticky
    Barbecue Sauce

1 At least 1 hour before smoke cooking, soak wood chunks in enough water to cover. Drain before using.

2 If desired, remove skin from chicken. For rub, in a small bowl stir together oregano, thyme, garlic salt, onion powder, and pepper. Sprinkle evenly over chicken; rub in with your fingers.

3 *In a smoker,* arrange preheated coals, half of the drained wood chunks, and the water pan according to the manufacturer's directions. Pour water into pan. Place chicken on the grill rack over water pan. Cover and smoke for 1½ to 2 hours or until chicken is tender and juices run clear. Add more coals, wood chunks, and water as needed. Remove chicken from smoker.

4 Meanwhile, prepare Sweet 'n' Sticky Barbecue Sauce. Generously brush some of the warm sauce over smoked chicken. Pass the remaining sauce.

Sweet 'n' Sticky Barbecue Sauce: In a small saucepan cook ½ cup finely chopped onion and 2 cloves garlic, minced, in 1 tablespoon hot olive oil until onion is tender. Stir in ¾ cup bottled chili sauce, ½ cup unsweetened pineapple juice, ¼ cup honey, 2 tablespoons Worcestershire sauce, and ½ teaspoon dry mustard. Bring to boiling; reduce heat. Simmer, uncovered, for 20 to 25 minutes or until sauce is desired consistency. Makes about 1¼ cups.

Nutrition Facts per serving: 535 cal., 29 g total fat (8 g sat. fat), 186 mg chol., 725 mg sodium, 25 g carbo., 2 g fiber, 43 g pro.
Daily Values: 10% vit. A, 22% vit. C, 6% calcium, 18% iron

Smoked Chicken Salad SMOKER

The blend of spices in this dressing and rub—thyme, mustard, onion, and, of course, ground red pepper—makes this chicken salad smokin'. Serve it with warm corn bread.

Soak: 1 hour **Prep:** 20 minutes **Smoke:** 45 minutes **Serves:** 4

4 cherry or apple wood
   chunks

Dressing:
2 tablespoons salad oil
2 tablespoons vinegar
1½ teaspoons sugar
1½ teaspoons snipped fresh
   thyme or ¼ teaspoon
   dried thyme, crushed
⅛ teaspoon dry mustard

Rub:
1 tablespoon salad oil
1 teaspoon onion powder
½ teaspoon black pepper
¼ teaspoon salt
¼ teaspoon ground red
   pepper

4 medium skinless, boneless
   chicken breast halves
   (about 1 pound total)
6 cups torn mixed salad
   greens
1 small green or red sweet
   pepper, cut into thin
   bite-size strips
1 pear, cored and thinly
   sliced
1 medium carrot, shredded
1 green onion, sliced

1 At least 1 hour before smoke cooking, soak wood chunks in enough water to cover. Drain before using.

2 For dressing, in a screw-top jar combine the 2 tablespoons oil, the vinegar, sugar, thyme, and dry mustard. Cover and shake well. Refrigerate until ready to serve.

3 For rub, in a small bowl combine the 1 tablespoon oil, the onion powder, black pepper, salt, and ground red pepper. Sprinkle mixture evenly over chicken; rub in with your fingers.

4 *In a smoker,* arrange preheated coals, drained wood chunks, and water pan according to the manufacturer's directions. Pour water into pan. Place chicken on the grill rack over water pan. Cover and smoke for 45 to 60 minutes or until chicken is tender and juices run clear. Remove chicken from smoker.

5 In a large salad bowl combine salad greens, sweet pepper, pear, carrot, and green onion. Cut chicken diagonally into strips; add to greens mixture. Shake the dressing and pour over greens mixture; toss gently to coat.

Nutrition Facts per serving: 272 cal., 12 g total fat (2 g sat. fat), 66 mg chol., 221 mg sodium, 14 g carbo., 3 g fiber, 28 g pro.
Daily Values: 97% vit. A, 45% vit. C, 6% calcium, 9% iron

Turkey with Wild Rice Dressing

If the Pilgrims had truly eaten turkey for the first Thanksgiving, it might have tasted something like this magnificent bird—tender and smoky from slow-cooking over a wood fire.

Soak: 1 hour **Prep:** 20 minutes **Smoke:** 2½ hours **Stand:** 15 minutes **Serves:** 8

4 cups hickory or alder
    wood chips

Dressing:
½ cup uncooked wild rice
2¼ cups water
½ cup uncooked brown rice
1 tablespoon instant chicken
    bouillon granules
½ teaspoon ground sage
2 cups sliced fresh
    mushrooms
1 medium onion, chopped
½ cup slivered almonds,
    toasted
4 slices bacon, crisp-cooked,
    drained, and crumbled

1 8- to 10-pound turkey
    Cooking oil
¼ cup currant jelly, melted

1 At least 1 hour before smoke cooking, soak wood chips in enough water to cover. Drain before using. For dressing, rinse wild rice. In a medium saucepan combine wild rice, water, brown rice, bouillon granules, and sage. Bring to boiling; reduce heat. Cover and simmer for 45 minutes. Stir in mushrooms and onion. Cook, covered, for 10 to 20 minutes more or until vegetables and rice are tender, stirring frequently. Stir in almonds and bacon.

2 Fold a 48×18-inch piece of heavy foil in half to make a 24×18-inch rectangle. Place dressing in center of foil. Bring up 2 opposite edges of foil and seal with a double fold. Fold remaining ends to completely enclose dressing, leaving space for steam to build. Refrigerate the packet until ready to cook.

3 Remove neck and giblets from turkey. Skewer neck skin to back. Twist wing tips under back. Tuck drumsticks under band of skin across tail or tie legs to tail with 100-percent-cotton string. Place turkey, breast side up, on a rack in a roasting pan. Brush turkey with cooking oil. Insert a meat thermometer into the center of an inside thigh muscle without touching bone.

4 *In a charcoal grill*, arrange medium-hot coals around edge of grill. Test for medium heat above center of grill. Sprinkle half of the drained wood chips over the coals. Place turkey in pan on the grill rack over center of grill. Cover and smoke for 2½ to 3 hours or until meat thermometer registers 180°. Place dressing packet next to turkey on grill rack directly over coals during the last 30 to 35 minutes of cooking. Add more coals and wood chips as needed. [*In a gas grill*, preheat grill. Reduce heat to medium. Adjust for indirect cooking (see page 6). Smoke as above, except add drained wood chips according to the manufacturer's directions.] Remove turkey and dressing from grill.

5 Brush turkey with jelly. Cover turkey with foil; let stand for 15 minutes before carving. Fluff dressing; serve with turkey.

Nutrition Facts per serving: 508 cal., 23 g total fat (6 g sat. fat), 125 mg chol., 483 mg sodium, 26 g carbo., 2 g fiber, 48 g pro.
Daily Values: 1% vit. C, 7% calcium, 20% iron

Double-Glazed Turkey Breasts ♥

Pull out this recipe if you're feeding a crowd that's divided on culinary preferences. Each turkey breast gets a distinctive glaze: one Asian-style; the other, honey-mustard. You really can please everyone.

Soak: 1 hour   **Prep:** 10 minutes   **Smoke:** 1¼ hours   **Stand:** 10 minutes   **Serves:** 8 to 10

4 cups hickory or mesquite wood chips

Five-Spice Glaze:
⅓ cup orange marmalade
1 tablespoon bottled hoisin sauce
¼ teaspoon five-spice powder
¼ teaspoon garlic powder

Honey-Mustard Glaze:
¼ cup honey
1 tablespoon Dijon-style mustard
1 tablespoon white wine Worcestershire sauce
1 tablespoon margarine or butter, melted

2 2- to 2½-pound turkey breast halves with bone
1 tablespoon cooking oil

1 At least 1 hour before smoke cooking, soak wood chips in enough water to cover. Drain before using.

2 For Five-Spice Glaze, in a small bowl stir together orange marmalade, hoisin sauce, five-spice powder, and garlic powder. Set aside.

3 For Honey-Mustard Glaze, in a small bowl stir together honey, mustard, Worcestershire sauce, and margarine. Set aside.

4 Remove bone from each breast half. Brush turkey with oil. Insert a meat thermometer into the center of one breast.

5 *In a charcoal grill*, arrange medium-hot coals around a drip pan. Test for medium heat above the pan. Sprinkle half of the drained wood chips over the coals. Place turkey breasts, side by side, on the grill rack over drip pan. Cover and smoke for 1¼ to 1½ hours or until meat thermometer registers 170°, brushing one breast with Five-Spice Glaze and the other breast with Honey-Mustard Glaze once during the last 15 minutes of cooking. Add more coals and wood chips as needed. [*In a gas grill*, preheat grill. Reduce heat to medium. Adjust for indirect cooking (see page 6). Add drained wood chips according to the manufacturer's directions. Smoke as above, except place turkey breasts, side by side, on a rack in a roasting pan.]

6 Remove turkey breasts from grill. Cover turkey with foil; let stand for 10 minutes before carving. To serve, slice the turkey breasts. Heat any of the remaining glazes and pass with turkey.

Nutrition Facts per serving: 253 cal., 10 g total fat (2 g sat. fat), 64 mg chol., 134 mg sodium, 19 g carbo., 1 g fiber, 22 g pro.
Daily Values: 1% vit. A, 2% vit. C, 3% calcium, 7% iron

Turkey with Raspberry Sauce ♥ SMOKER

A double dose of fruit gives this all-white-meat feature its appeal. Orange wood imparts the turkey breast with its citrusy-smoky taste, and fresh raspberry sauce sweetens the deal.

Soak: 1 hour **Prep:** 10 minutes **Smoke:** 2 hours **Stand:** 10 minutes **Serves:** 4 or 5

8 to 10 orange, apple, or
    peach wood chunks

Sauce:
½ cup seedless raspberry jam
4 teaspoons Dijon-style
    mustard
1 teaspoon finely shredded
    orange peel
1 cup fresh or frozen
    raspberries, thawed

1 2- to 2½-pound turkey
    breast half with bone

1 At least 1 hour before smoke cooking, soak wood chunks in enough water to cover. Drain before using.

2 For sauce, in a small bowl stir together raspberry jam, mustard, and orange peel. Transfer ¼ cup of the sauce to another bowl for basting. Stir raspberries into the remaining sauce. Cover and refrigerate until ready to serve.

3 If desired, remove skin from turkey. Insert a meat thermometer into the center of turkey without touching bone.

4 *In a smoker,* arrange preheated coals, half of the drained wood chunks, and the water pan according to the manufacturer's directions. Pour water into pan. Place turkey, bone side down, on the grill rack over water pan. Cover and smoke for 2 to 2½ hours or until meat thermometer registers 170°, brushing once with basting sauce during the last 15 minutes of cooking. Add more coals, wood chunks, and water as needed. Discard any remaining basting sauce.

5 Remove turkey from smoker. Cover turkey with foil; let stand for 10 minutes before carving. Serve turkey with reserved sauce.

Nutrition Facts per serving: 220 cal., 7 g total fat (2 g sat. fat), 64 mg chol., 65 mg sodium, 16 g carbo., 1 g fiber, 22 g pro.
Daily Values: 1% vit. A, 10% vit. C, 3% calcium, 8% iron

Barbecued Turkey Tenderloins ♥ SMOKER

Tahini—sesame butter—adds a rich, nutty flavor to a purchased barbecue sauce. Look for it at health food stores or Middle Eastern food markets if you can't find it at your supermarket.

Soak: 1 hour **Prep:** 15 minutes **Smoke:** 1¼ hours **Serves:** 4

6 to 8 hickory or oak wood chunks

Sauce:
½ cup bottled hickory barbecue sauce
1 small fresh jalapeño pepper, seeded and finely chopped
1 tablespoon tahini (sesame butter)

4 tomatillos, husked and halved lengthwise, or ½ cup salsa verde
2 turkey breast tenderloins (about 1 pound total)
4 French-style rolls, split and toasted
Spinach leaves

1 At least 1 hour before smoke cooking, soak wood chunks in enough water to cover. Drain before using.

2 For sauce, in a small bowl combine barbecue sauce, jalapeño pepper, and tahini. Transfer half of the sauce to another bowl and reserve until ready to serve. If using tomatillos, thread them onto metal skewers. Set aside.

3 *In a smoker,* arrange preheated coals, half of the drained wood chunks, and the water pan according to the manufacturer's directions. Pour water into pan. Brush both sides of turkey with the remaining sauce. Place turkey on the grill rack over water pan. Cover and smoke for 1¼ to 1½ hours or until turkey is tender and juices run clear. Place tomatillos next to turkey on grill rack directly over coals during the last 20 minutes of cooking. Add more coals, wood chunks, and water as needed. Remove turkey and tomatillos from smoker. Thinly slice the turkey and chop the tomatillos.

4 To serve, in a small saucepan cook and stir the reserved sauce over low heat until heated through. Remove from heat. Fill the toasted rolls with a few spinach leaves, the smoked turkey, and tomatillos or salsa verde. Top with the reserved sauce.

Nutrition Facts per serving: 303 cal., 5 g total fat (1 g sat. fat), 68 mg chol., 695 mg sodium, 32 g carbo., 1 g fiber, 31 g pro.
Daily Values: 2% vit. A, 15% vit. C, 6% calcium, 14% iron

Chili-Rubbed Drumsticks ♥ SMOKER

Free your inner barbarian—and feast on fun-to-eat turkey drumsticks! Wisps of smoke and hot-and-spicy seasonings give the turkey a bonanza of lip-tingling flavor.

Soak: 1 hour **Prep:** 5 minutes **Smoke:** 2½ hours **Serves:** 6

8 to 10 hickory wood
    chunks

Rub:

1 tablespoon chili powder
1 tablespoon finely
    shredded lime peel
1½ teaspoons ground cumin
½ teaspoon salt

6 turkey drumsticks (3 to
    4½ pounds total)
    Bottled salsa or barbecue
    sauce (optional)

1 At least 1 hour before smoke cooking, soak wood chunks in enough water to cover. Drain before using.

2 For rub, in a small bowl combine chili powder, lime peel, cumin, and salt. Sprinkle mixture evenly over turkey; rub in with your fingers.

3 *In a smoker*, arrange preheated coals, half of the drained wood chunks, and the water pan according to the manufacturer's directions. Pour water into pan. Place turkey on the grill rack over water pan. Cover and smoke for 2½ to 3 hours or until turkey is tender and juices run clear. Add more coals, wood chunks, and water as needed. If desired, serve the turkey with salsa.

Nutrition Facts per serving: 178 cal., 9 g total fat (3 g sat. fat), 80 mg chol., 269 mg sodium, 1 g carbo., 1 g fiber, 22 g pro.
Daily Values: 9% vit. A, 4% vit. C, 4% calcium, 11% iron

handling chile peppers

Both in the Test Kitchen and my own kitchen, I work with a lot of chile peppers. I love the taste of them, but I don't want their hot oils on my hands. I always wear plastic gloves or small plastic bags on my hands when seeding and chopping chiles. The seeds are the hottest part of the pepper, so take care to avoid handling them—and be sure to wash your hands thoroughly when you're done.

Lori Wilson

Test Kitchen Home Economist

Duck with Honey-Thyme Sauce ♥

The dark, moist flesh of duck lends itself beautifully to smoking. Serve succulent slices over couscous studded with lightly steamed asparagus, cherry tomato wedges, and chopped toasted hazelnuts.

Prep: 15 minutes **Marinate:** 2 hours **Smoke:** 1 hour **Serves:** 4

2 skinless, boneless domestic duck breast halves (about 1½ pounds total)

Marinade:
⅔ cup chicken broth
⅓ cup honey
1 shallot, finely chopped
1 tablespoon snipped fresh lemon thyme or regular thyme
2 cloves garlic, minced
1 teaspoon white wine vinegar
¼ teaspoon salt
⅛ teaspoon pepper

4 cups orange or apple wood chips
Fresh lemon thyme or regular thyme sprigs

1 Place duck in a plastic bag set in a shallow dish. For marinade, in a small bowl combine chicken broth, honey, shallot, the snipped thyme, the garlic, wine vinegar, salt, and pepper. Pour half of the marinade over duck; seal bag. Marinate in the refrigerator for 2 to 24 hours, turning bag occasionally. Cover the remaining marinade and store in the refrigerator to use as sauce.

2 At least 1 hour before smoke cooking, soak wood chips in enough water to cover. Drain before using. Drain duck, reserving marinade.

3 *In a charcoal grill*, arrange medium-hot coals around a drip pan. Test for medium heat above the pan. Sprinkle half of the drained wood chips and the thyme sprigs over the coals. Place duck on the grill rack over drip pan. Cover and smoke about 1 hour or until duck is tender and juices run clear, brushing once with marinade halfway through cooking. Add more coals and wood chips as needed. [*In a gas grill*, preheat grill. Reduce heat to medium. Adjust for indirect cooking (see page 6). Smoke as above, except add drained wood chips according to the manufacturer's directions.] Discard the remaining marinade. Remove duck from grill.

4 Meanwhile, for sauce, in a small saucepan bring the reserved marinade to boiling; reduce heat. Simmer, uncovered, about 5 minutes or until reduced to ⅓ cup. Remove from heat. If desired, remove skin and fat from duck. Slice duck and serve with sauce.

Nutrition Facts per serving: 144 cal., 3 g total fat (1 g sat. fat), 136 mg chol., 256 mg sodium, 2 g carbo., 0 g fiber, 27 g pro.
Daily Values: 1% vit. A, 7% vit. C, 1% calcium, 25% iron

Fish & Seafood

Honey-Bourbon Salmon

In This Chapter:

Red Snapper with Crab Stuffing

Mom always told you it was what was on the inside that counted—and in the case of this elegant fish dish, that couldn't be more true: a sweet crabmeat filling enriched by sautéed mushrooms.

Soak: 1 hour **Prep:** 10 minutes **Smoke:** 45 minutes **Serves:** 6

2 cups mesquite or hickory wood chips
1 3-pound or two 1½-pound fresh or frozen dressed red snapper (with head and tail)

Stuffing:
1 cup sliced fresh mushrooms
2 tablespoons margarine or butter
1 pound lump crabmeat or two 6-ounce cans crabmeat, drained

Sauce:
2 tablespoons olive oil or cooking oil
1 tablespoon lime juice
⅛ teaspoon garlic powder

Rub:
1 tablespoon seafood seasoning
1 teaspoon sugar
1 teaspoon black pepper
¾ teaspoon onion salt
¾ teaspoon ground ginger
¾ teaspoon ground cinnamon
¾ teaspoon crushed red pepper
¼ teaspoon salt
⅛ teaspoon ground cloves

1 At least 1 hour before smoke cooking, soak wood chips in enough water to cover. Drain before using. Thaw fish, if frozen. For stuffing, cook mushrooms in margarine until tender. Remove from heat. Break up crabmeat into bite-size pieces, removing any cartilage. Stir crabmeat into mushrooms; set aside.

2 For sauce, in a small bowl combine oil, lime juice, and garlic powder; set aside. For rub, in a small bowl combine seafood seasoning, sugar, black pepper, onion salt, ginger, cinnamon, red pepper, salt, and cloves; set aside.

3 Rinse fish; pat dry with paper towels. Spoon the stuffing into the fish cavity. Skewer the cavity closed with wooden toothpicks. Brush fish with some of the sauce. Sprinkle rub evenly over fish; rub in with your fingers. Place fish on a greased 18×12-inch piece of heavy foil.

4 Fold a 24×18-inch piece of heavy foil in half to make an 18×12-inch rectangle. Place any remaining stuffing in center of foil. Bring up 2 opposite edges of foil and seal with a double fold. Fold remaining ends to completely enclose stuffing, leaving space for steam to build. Refrigerate packet until ready to cook.

5 *In a charcoal grill,* arrange medium-hot coals around a drip pan. Test for medium heat above the pan. Sprinkle the drained wood chips over the coals. Place fish on foil on the grill rack over drip pan. Cover and smoke until fish flakes easily when tested with a fork, brushing once with sauce halfway through cooking. (Allow 45 to 55 minutes for large fish or 35 to 45 minutes for smaller fish.) Place stuffing packet next to fish on grill rack directly over coals during the last 15 minutes of cooking. [*In a gas grill,* preheat grill. Reduce heat to medium. Adjust for indirect cooking (see page 6). Smoke as above, except add drained wood chips according to the manufacturer's directions.] Discard any remaining sauce. Remove toothpicks.

Nutrition Facts per serving: 354 cal., 13 g total fat (2 g sat. fat), 145 mg chol., 674 mg sodium, 3 g carbo., 1 g fiber, 55 g pro.
Daily Values: 9% vit. A, 11% vit. C, 16% calcium, 9% iron

Fennel-Stuffed Trout SMOKER

Perhaps because of its origin as a shoreside delicacy, fresh trout is especially good cooked over a smoky fire. Serve this freshwater fish with a mixture of new potatoes, zucchini, and red peppers.

Soak: 1 hour **Prep:** 10 minutes **Smoke:** 1½ hours **Serves:** 4

6 to 8 alder or pecan wood chunks

4 8- to 10-ounce fresh or frozen dressed trout or other fish

Stuffing:

2 fennel bulbs

1 clove garlic, minced

¼ teaspoon salt

⅛ teaspoon pepper

2 tablespoons margarine or butter

1 tablespoon snipped fresh parsley

Sauce:

3 tablespoons margarine or butter

1 tablespoon lemon juice

½ teaspoon dried rosemary, crushed

Dash pepper

Lemon wedges (optional)

1 At least 1 hour before smoke cooking, soak wood chunks in enough water to cover. Drain before using.

2 Thaw fish, if frozen. For stuffing, cut off and discard upper stalks of fennel. Remove any wilted outer layers; cut off a thin slice from bases. Chop fennel bulbs (should have about 2½ cups). In a medium saucepan cook and stir fennel, garlic, salt, and the ⅛ teaspoon pepper in the 2 tablespoons margarine about 10 minutes or until fennel is tender. Stir in parsley; set aside.

3 For sauce, in a small saucepan combine the 3 tablespoons margarine, the lemon juice, rosemary, and the dash pepper. Heat through.

4 Rinse fish; pat dry with paper towels. Spoon the stuffing into the fish cavities. Skewer the cavities closed with wooden toothpicks. Brush fish with some of the sauce.

5 *In a smoker*, arrange preheated coals, half of the drained wood chunks, and the water pan according to the manufacturer's directions. Pour water into pan. Place fish on the greased grill rack over water pan. Cover and smoke for 1½ to 2 hours or until fish flakes easily when tested with a fork, brushing once with sauce halfway through cooking. Add more coals, wood chunks, and water as needed. Discard any remaining sauce.

6 Remove the toothpicks from fish. If desired, serve fish with lemon wedges.

Nutrition Facts per serving: 306 cal., 20 g total fat (4 g sat. fat), 67 mg chol., 386 mg sodium, 6 g carbo., 17 g fiber, 25 g pro.
Daily Values: 19% vit. A, 23% vit. C, 12% calcium, 3% iron

Tropical Halibut Steaks ♥ SMOKER

Toasting the coconut for this tropically inclined entrée heightens its sweet, nutty flavor. Simply bake the coconut in a 350° oven about 10 minutes, stirring once, until it's golden brown.

Soak: 1 hour **Prep:** 15 minutes **Smoke:** 45 minutes **Serves:** 4

4 apple or orange wood
    chunks
4 6-ounce fresh or frozen
    halibut steaks, cut
    1 inch thick
Marinade:
    ⅓ cup pineapple-orange juice
    ⅓ cup soy sauce
    ¼ teaspoon curry powder
Sauce:
    1 8-ounce can pineapple
        chunks (juice pack)
    ¼ of a medium cantaloupe
        or ½ of a papaya
        Dash curry powder
    2 teaspoons cornstarch

    2 tablespoons coconut,
        toasted

1 At least 1 hour before smoke cooking, soak wood chunks in enough water to cover. Drain before using.

2 Thaw fish, if frozen. Rinse fish; pat dry with paper towels. Place fish in a plastic bag set in a shallow dish. For marinade, in a small bowl combine pineapple-orange juice, soy sauce, and the ¼ teaspoon curry powder.

3 Pour marinade over fish; seal bag. Marinate in the refrigerator for 1 hour, turning bag occasionally.

4 Meanwhile, for sauce, drain pineapple, reserving juice. Peel and seed cantaloupe or papaya. Finely chop pineapple and cantaloupe or papaya. In a small saucepan combine the chopped fruit and the dash curry powder. Add enough water to the reserved pineapple juice to make ½ cup liquid. Stir in cornstarch; add to the fruit mixture. Cook and stir over medium heat until thickened and bubbly. Cook and stir for 2 minutes more. Remove from heat; set aside. Drain fish, reserving marinade.

5 *In a smoker,* arrange preheated coals, drained wood chunks, and water pan according to the manufacturer's directions. Pour water into pan. Place fish on the greased grill rack over water pan. Cover and smoke for 45 to 60 minutes or until fish flakes easily when tested with a fork, brushing once with marinade halfway through cooking. Discard the remaining marinade.

6 To serve, reheat the sauce and spoon over fish. Sprinkle the fish with toasted coconut.

Nutrition Facts per serving: 262 cal., 5 g total fat (1 g sat. fat), 54 mg chol., 740 mg sodium, 16 g carbo., 1 g fiber, 38 g pro.
Daily Values: 26% vit. A, 35% vit. C, 9% calcium, 10% iron

Smoky Bass with Carambola Salsa ♥

Carambola—also called star fruit because of its resemblance to those heavenly bodies when cut crosswise—thrives in tropical climates. Its flavor ranges from sweet to tart.

Soak: 1 hour **Prep:** 10 minutes **Smoke:** 45 minutes **Serves:** 4

2 cups orange, apple, or cherry wood chips

4 4-ounce fresh or frozen sea bass or red snapper fillets, about 1 inch thick

Salsa:

½ to 1 teaspoon cumin seed

3 large carambola (star fruit)

1 small lime

½ of a small fresh poblano pepper, seeded and finely chopped

2 tablespoons snipped fresh cilantro

½ teaspoon salt

¼ teaspoon ground red pepper

1 At least 1 hour before smoke cooking, soak wood chips in enough water to cover. Drain before using.

2 Thaw fish, if frozen. For salsa, in a dry skillet cook cumin seed, uncovered, over medium-high heat for 1 to 2 minutes or until toasted, shaking the skillet frequently. Set aside.

3 Slice 1 carambola; cover and refrigerate for garnish. Chop the remaining carambola. Finely shred the lime peel. Set aside. Peel, section, and chop lime. In a small bowl combine cumin seed, chopped carambola, chopped lime, poblano pepper, cilantro, and ⅛ teaspoon of the salt. Cover and refrigerate until ready to serve.

4 Rinse fish; pat dry with paper towels. Sprinkle with the lime peel, the remaining salt, and ground red pepper.

5 *In a charcoal grill*, arrange medium-hot coals around a drip pan. Test for medium heat above the pan. Sprinkle the drained wood chips over the coals. Place fish on the greased grill rack over drip pan, tucking under any thin edges. Cover and smoke for 45 to 60 minutes or until fish flakes easily when tested with a fork. [*In a gas grill*, preheat grill. Reduce heat to medium. Adjust for indirect cooking (see page 6). Smoke as above, except add drained wood chips according to manufacturer's directions.]

6 Serve the fish with salsa. Garnish fish with the reserved sliced carambola.

Nutrition Facts per serving: 143 cal., 3 g total fat (1 g sat. fat), 47 mg chol., 280 mg sodium, 8 g carbo., 1 g fiber, 22 g pro.
Daily Values: 10% vit. A, 54% vit. C, 2% calcium, 5% iron

Salmon with Horseradish Cream SMOKER

"If a little is good, then more is better" isn't always a good culinary proposition (think hot peppers or aromatic bitters). But in this case, a double dose of smoke is what makes the fish taste so good.

Soak: 1 hour **Prep:** 5 minutes **Smoke:** 45 minutes **Serves:** 4

4 hickory, alder, or apple wood chunks

4 6-ounce fresh or frozen salmon fillets (with skin), about 1 inch thick

4 slices smoked salmon (about 3 ounces)

2 tablespoons snipped fresh dill

1 tablespoon lemon juice

Sauce:

½ cup dairy sour cream

4 teaspoons prepared horseradish

1 green onion, thinly sliced

1 At least 1 hour before smoke cooking, soak wood chunks in enough water to cover. Drain before using.

2 Thaw fish, if frozen. Rinse fish; pat dry with paper towels. Make a pocket in each fish fillet by cutting horizontally from one side almost to the other side. Fill with slices of smoked salmon and 2 teaspoons of the dill, folding salmon slices as necessary to fit. Brush the fish with lemon juice and top with 2 teaspoons of the dill. Sprinkle with salt and pepper.

3 *In a smoker,* arrange preheated coals, drained wood chunks, and water pan according to the manufacturer's directions. Pour water into pan. Place fish, skin side down, on the greased grill rack over water pan. Cover and smoke about 45 minutes or until fish flakes easily when tested with a fork.

4 Meanwhile, for sauce, in a small bowl combine the sour cream, horseradish, green onion, and the remaining dill. Serve the fish with sauce.

Nutrition Facts per serving: 245 cal., 13 g total fat (5 g sat. fat), 48 mg chol., 337 mg sodium, 2 g carbo., 0 g fiber, 29 g pro.
Daily Values: 11% vit. A, 6% vit. C, 4% calcium, 9% iron

flavor boosters

Smoke will infuse whatever you're cooking with wonderful flavor, but I like to experiment with other flavoring agents, too. Consider adding another liquid—such as wine, fruit juice, or marinade—to the water in the smoker pan. Herbs and spices can also be added to the water pan, as well as to the coals. I like to include a couple of heads of garlic, bay leaves, or orange peel in the coals when I'm smoke cooking.

Jill Moberly

Test Kitchen Home Economist

Honey-Bourbon Salmon

Simple but sophisticated, this sweet-and-spicy salmon gets great flavor and aroma from a splash of bourbon in the marinade. Serve it with steamed asparagus and a tossed salad.

Soak: 1 hour **Prep:** 10 minutes **Smoke:** 45 minutes **Serves:** 4

2 cups apple or alder wood chips
4 6-ounce fresh or frozen salmon steaks, cut 1 inch thick

Marinade:
¾ cup bourbon
½ cup packed brown sugar
2 tablespoons honey
2 teaspoons soy sauce
½ teaspoon ground ginger
¼ teaspoon pepper

1 At least 1 hour before smoke cooking, soak wood chips in enough water to cover. Drain before using.

2 Thaw fish, if frozen. Rinse fish; pat dry with paper towels. Place fish in a plastic bag set in a shallow dish. For marinade, combine bourbon, brown sugar, honey, soy sauce, ginger, and pepper. Pour over fish; seal bag. Marinate in the refrigerator for 1 hour, turning bag occasionally. Drain fish, reserving marinade.

3 *In a charcoal grill*, arrange medium-hot coals around a drip pan. Test for medium heat above the pan. Sprinkle the drained wood chips over the coals. Place fish on the greased grill rack over drip pan. Cover and smoke for 45 to 60 minutes or until fish flakes easily when tested with a fork. [*In a gas grill*, preheat grill. Reduce heat to medium. Adjust for indirect cooking (see page 6). Smoke as above, except add drained wood chips according to the manufacturer's directions.] Remove from grill.

4 Meanwhile, cook marinade, uncovered, for 5 to 10 minutes or until slightly thickened. Before serving, brush marinade over fish.

Nutrition Facts per serving: 402 cal., 15 g total fat (3 g sat. fat), 105 mg chol., 162 mg sodium, 18 g carbo., 0 g fiber, 36 g pro.
Daily Values: 6% vit. A, 2% calcium, 7% iron

Raspberry-Shrimp Salad

With lightly smoked shrimp and plump raspberries, this refreshing salad makes your table pretty in pink! Simply add some crusty rolls and a luscious chocolate dessert for an alfresco dinner with friends.

Soak: 1 hour **Prep:** 10 minutes **Smoke:** 10 minutes **Serves:** 4

2 cups orange or peach wood chips
1 pound fresh or frozen jumbo shrimp in shells (12 to 16)

Vinaigrette:
1 cup fresh raspberries
¼ cup olive oil or salad oil
¼ cup white wine vinegar or white vinegar
1 teaspoon sugar
1 teaspoon finely shredded orange peel
¼ teaspoon dry mustard

1 cup fresh pea pods
6 cups torn red-tipped leaf lettuce
1 cup fresh raspberries

1 At least 1 hour before smoke cooking, soak wood chips and 8 short wooden skewers in enough water to cover. Drain before using.

2 Thaw shrimp, if frozen. For vinaigrette, in a blender container or food processor bowl combine 1 cup raspberries, the oil, vinegar, sugar, orange peel, and dry mustard. Cover and blend or process until smooth; set aside.

3 Remove tips and strings from pea pods. In a small covered saucepan cook pea pods in a small amount of boiling water for 2 to 4 minutes or until crisp-tender. Drain; set aside. Peel and devein shrimp, leaving tails intact. Rinse shrimp; pat dry with paper towels. Loosely thread shrimp onto soaked skewers.

4 *In a charcoal grill,* arrange medium-hot coals around a drip pan. Test for medium heat above the pan. Sprinkle the drained wood chips over the coals. Place skewers on the greased grill rack over drip pan. Cover and smoke for 10 to 12 minutes or until shrimp are opaque. [*In a gas grill*, preheat grill. Reduce heat to medium. Adjust for indirect cooking (see page 6). Smoke as above, except add drained wood chips according to the manufacturer's directions.]

5 To serve, arrange the torn lettuce and pea pods on 4 dinner plates. Divide the smoked shrimp among the plates. Top with the remaining 1 cup raspberries. Serve with vinaigrette.

Nutrition Facts per serving: 271 cal., 16 g total fat (2 g sat. fat), 129 mg chol., 135 mg sodium, 13 g carbo., 6 g fiber, 19 g pro.
Daily Values: 37% vit. A, 70% vit. C, 12% calcium, 21% iron

Brie-Stuffed Lobster Tails

It doesn't get any better than this! With each bite, creamy, nutty-flavored Brie melts into the smoky-sweet meat of lobster tail. Uncork some champagne and serve this the next time you're celebrating.

Soak: 1 hour **Prep:** 10 minutes **Smoke:** 16 minutes **Serves:** 4

2 cups alder or apple wood chips
4 5-ounce fresh or frozen rock lobster tails

Stuffing:
2 tablespoons chopped onion
1 tablespoon margarine or butter
1 cup soft bread crumbs (about 1½ slices)
1 ounce chopped Brie or shredded Monterey Jack cheese
1 tablespoon snipped fresh parsley

¼ cup margarine or butter, melted

1 At least 1 hour before smoke cooking, soak wood chips in enough water to cover. Drain before using.

2 Thaw lobster, if frozen. For stuffing, in a small saucepan cook onion in the 1 tablespoon margarine until tender. Stir in bread crumbs, cheese, and parsley. Set aside.

3 Rinse lobster; pat dry with paper towels. To butterfly each lobster tail, use kitchen scissors or a sharp knife to cut lengthwise through center of hard top shell and meat. Cut to, but not through, bottom shell. Press the shell halves apart with your fingers. Brush lobster meat with some of the melted margarine.

4 *In a charcoal grill,* arrange medium-hot coals around a drip pan. Test for medium heat above the pan. Sprinkle the drained wood chips over the coals. Place lobster tails, meat side down, on the greased grill rack over drip pan. Cover and smoke for 10 minutes. Remove from grill.

5 Brush lobster meat with the remaining melted margarine. Lightly pack the stuffing into lobster cavities. Return to grill, stuffing side up. Cover and smoke for 6 to 8 minutes more or until lobster meat is opaque. [*In a gas grill,* preheat grill. Reduce heat to medium. Adjust for indirect cooking (see page 6). Smoke as above, except add drained wood chips according to the manufacturer's directions.]

Nutrition Facts per serving: 252 cal., 17 g total fat (4 g sat. fat), 81 mg chol., 501 mg sodium, 7 g carbo., 0 g fiber, 17 g pro.
Daily Values: 16% vit. A, 3% vit. C, 7% calcium, 4% iron

Kansas City Barbecue Rub

Sauces, Rubs & Marinades

Honey-Mustard Sauce

Sweet and Spunky Barbecue Sauce

In This Chapter:

Sweet and Spunky Barbecue Sauce

This is it—a great basic barbecue sauce that doesn't come in a bottle. It takes just 10 minutes to stir it together and a half hour to bubble on the stove. Try it on beef, lamb, pork, or poultry.

Prep: 10 minutes **Cook:** 30 minutes **Yield:** about 1½ cups (enough for 12 servings)

1 cup catsup
½ cup water
1 small onion, chopped
¼ cup Worcestershire sauce
¼ cup cider vinegar
2 tablespoons brown sugar
2 tablespoons molasses
2 teaspoons dry mustard
1 teaspoon garlic powder
1 teaspoon chili powder
¼ teaspoon ground red pepper
¼ teaspoon lemon juice

1 In a large saucepan combine the catsup, water, onion, Worcestershire sauce, vinegar, brown sugar, molasses, mustard, garlic powder, chili powder, ground red pepper, and lemon juice. Bring to boiling; reduce heat. Simmer, uncovered, for 30 minutes, stirring occasionally.

2 To use, brush beef, lamb, pork, or poultry once or twice with sauce during the last 10 to 15 minutes of smoke cooking. If desired, reheat and pass additional sauce. To store any remaining sauce, cover and refrigerate up to 2 weeks.

Nutrition Facts per 2 tablespoons: 45 cal., 0 g total fat (0 g sat. fat), 0 mg chol., 297 mg sodium, 11 g carbo., 1 g fiber, 1 g pro.
Daily Values: 6% vit. A, 7% vit. C, 2% calcium, 4% iron

Honey-Mustard Sauce

The presence of honey and apple cider in this 10-minute sauce makes it a natural for glazing pork or poultry. Increase the amount of ground red pepper slightly if you like a little fire with your smoke.

Prep: 5 minutes **Cook:** 5 minutes **Yield:** about ½ cup (enough for 8 servings)

⅓ cup honey
3 tablespoons Dijon-style mustard
2 tablespoons finely chopped onion or 2 teaspoons dried minced onion
2 tablespoons apple cider or apple juice
⅛ teaspoon ground red pepper

1 For sauce, in a small saucepan combine honey, mustard, onion, apple cider, and ground red pepper. Bring to boiling; reduce heat. Simmer, uncovered, for 5 to 7 minutes or until sauce is slightly thickened.

2 To use, brush meat, poultry, or fish once or twice with sauce during the last 10 to 15 minutes of smoke cooking. If desired, reheat and pass any remaining sauce.

Nutrition Facts per tablespoon: 53 cal., 0 g total fat (0 g sat. fat), 0 mg chol., 143 mg sodium, 12 g carbo., 0 g fiber, 0 g pro.

Hot Asian Barbecue Sauce

Sesame oil comes two ways: The light-colored sesame oil is light in flavor and is best used in salad dressings. Toasted, or Asian, sesame oil is dark brown and has a rich sesame flavor.

Prep: 10 minutes **Yield:** about 3 cups (enough for 24 servings)

½ cup bottled hoisin sauce
½ cup honey
3 tablespoons soy sauce
2 to 3 tablespoons sesame seed, toasted
4 teaspoons finely shredded orange peel
1 fresh jalapeño or serrano pepper, chopped
1 tablespoon dry sherry
1 tablespoon orange liqueur (optional)
2 teaspoons finely shredded lemon or lime peel
1 teaspoon grated fresh ginger
1 teaspoon toasted sesame oil
1 clove garlic, minced

1 In a medium bowl combine hoisin sauce, honey, soy sauce, sesame seed, orange peel, jalapeño pepper, sherry, orange liqueur (if desired), lemon peel, ginger, sesame oil, and garlic.

2 To use, brush meat, poultry, or fish once or twice with sauce during the last 10 to 15 minutes of smoke cooking. If desired, heat and pass additional sauce. To store any remaining sauce, cover and refrigerate up to 2 weeks.

Nutrition Facts per 2 tablespoons: 45 cal., 1 g total fat (0 g sat. fat), 0 mg chol., 220 mg sodium, 9 g carbo., 0 g fiber, 0 g pro.
Daily Values: 2% vit. C, 1% calcium, 1% iron

Super-Fast Barbecue Sauce

The sweet of apricot preserves and the savory of soy sauce and onion give bottled barbecue sauce a flavor boost in record time.

Prep: 10 minutes **Yield:** about 1¼ cups (enough for 10 servings)

¾ cup apricot preserves
½ cup bottled barbecue sauce
2 tablespoons regular or reduced-sodium soy sauce
1 tablespoon dried minced onion

1 Snip any large pieces of apricot preserves. In a small saucepan stir together preserves, barbecue sauce, soy sauce, and onion. Cook and stir over medium heat until heated through.

2 To use, brush beef, lamb, pork, or poultry once or twice with sauce during the last 10 to 15 minutes of smoke cooking. If desired, reheat and pass the remaining sauce.

Nutrition Facts per 2 tablespoons: 78 cal., 0 g total fat (0 g sat. fat), 0 mg chol., 310 mg sodium, 19 g carbo., 0 g fiber, 0 g pro.
Daily Values: 2% vit. C, 2% iron

Kansas City Barbecue Rub

All the barbecue hot spots—St. Louis, Austin, and Memphis, to name a few—have their own way of doing things. This is the way Kansas City folks like their rub—spicy and a little sweet.

Prep: 5 minutes **Yield:** about ⅔ cup (enough for 6 to 8 pounds meat or poultry)

¼ cup sugar
1 tablespoon seasoned salt
1 tablespoon garlic salt
1 tablespoon paprika
1 tablespoon barbecue seasoning
1½ teaspoons onion salt
1½ teaspoons celery salt
1½ teaspoons chili powder
1½ teaspoons black pepper
¾ teaspoon ground ginger
¾ teaspoon lemon-pepper seasoning
¼ teaspoon ground thyme
⅛ teaspoon ground red pepper

1 In a small bowl combine sugar, seasoned salt, garlic salt, paprika, barbecue seasoning, onion salt, celery salt, chili powder, black pepper, ginger, lemon-pepper seasoning, thyme, and ground red pepper.

2 To use, sprinkle mixture evenly over meat or poultry; rub in with your fingers. Smoke meat or poultry.

Nutrition Facts per teaspoon: 9 cal., 0 g total fat (0 g sat. fat), 0 mg chol., 480 mg sodium, 2 g carbo., 0 g fiber, 0 g pro.
Daily Values: 2% vit. A, 1% calcium, 1% iron

Spanish Olive Rub

This piquant Sicilian-style rub is great on the outside of smoked foods—or on the inside. Try tucking it into a pocket cut into a steak or chop before smoke cooking.

Prep: 5 minutes **Yield:** about ⅓ cup (enough for 1 to 1½ pounds meat, poultry, or fish)

½ cup pimiento-stuffed green olives
1 tablespoon capers, drained
3 cloves garlic, chopped
1½ teaspoons finely shredded orange peel
½ teaspoon pepper

1 In a blender container or food processor bowl combine olives, capers, garlic, orange peel, and pepper. Cover and blend or process until mixture is chunky.

2 To use, sprinkle mixture evenly over meat, poultry, or fish; rub in with your fingers. Smoke meat, poultry, or fish.

Nutrition Facts per tablespoon: 20 cal., 2 g total fat (0 g sat. fat), 0 mg chol., 375 mg sodium, 1 g carbo., 0 g fiber, 0 g pro.
Daily Values: 1% vit. A, 2% vit. C, 1% calcium, 2% iron

Fruit Salsa

This colorful salsa adds fresh taste and eye appeal to all sorts of smoked foods—meaty fish in particular. Try it with halibut, shark, or salmon.

Prep: 25 minutes **Chill:** 8 hours **Yield:** about 2 cups (enough for 8 servings)

1   cup chopped papaya or mango
1   cup finely chopped fresh pineapple
¼   cup finely slivered red onion
¼   cup slivered yellow, orange, and/or green sweet pepper
3   tablespoons snipped fresh cilantro
1   teaspoon finely shredded lime or lemon peel
2   tablespoons lime or lemon juice
2 to 4 teaspoons finely chopped fresh jalapeño pepper
1   teaspoon grated fresh ginger

1 In a medium bowl stir together the papaya, pineapple, red onion, sweet pepper, cilantro, lime peel, lime juice, jalapeño pepper, and ginger.

2 Cover and refrigerate for 8 to 24 hours to blend flavors. Serve with smoked meat, poultry, fish, or seafood.

Nutrition Facts per ¼ cup: 22 cal., 0 g total fat (0 g sat. fat), 0 mg chol., 2 mg sodium, 6 g carbo., 1 g fiber, 0 g pro.
Daily Values: 4% vit. A, 49% vit. C, 1% calcium, 1% iron

Cranberry and Apricot Chutney

Try this refreshing chutney with smoked pork loin, a holiday ham, or thick, juicy pork chops. It can be made up to 4 days ahead—just cover it tightly and store it in the refrigerator.

Prep: 15 minutes **Cook:** 5 minutes **Yield:** about 3½ cups (enough for 14 servings)

1¼ cups granulated sugar
½ cup water
1 12-ounce package
   cranberries
¾ cup snipped dried apricots
3 tablespoons brown sugar
3 tablespoons cider vinegar
1 tablespoon minced fresh
   ginger

1 In a heavy large saucepan combine granulated sugar and water. Cook and stir over medium-high heat until sugar is dissolved. Bring to boiling without stirring. Stir in cranberries, apricots, brown sugar, vinegar, and ginger; reduce heat. Simmer, uncovered, about 5 minutes or until cranberries have popped and mixture starts to thicken. Remove from heat; cool.

2 Serve the chutney with smoked meat, poultry, fish, or seafood. To store any remaining chutney, cover and refrigerate up to 4 days. Before serving, let stand at room temperature for 30 minutes.

Nutrition Facts per ¼ cup: 103 cal., 0 g total fat (0 g sat. fat), 0 mg chol., 2 mg sodium, 27 g carbo., 2 g fiber, 0 g pro.
Daily Values: 10% vit. A, 6% vit. C, 1% calcium, 2% iron

india's favorite condiment

In America, catsup may be the condiment of choice; in India, it's chutney. Chutney is a mixture of fruit, vinegar, sugar, and spices. Its texture can be chunky or smooth; its flavor ranges from mild to fiery. In its land of origin, it's served most often as an accompaniment to curries. It's also delicious with smoked meats and cheeses.

Tarragon-Wine Marinade

Fresh tarragon has a delightful licorice-like flavor. Try stirring a little into honey-mustard to make a quick dipping sauce for smoked foods.

Prep: 5 minutes **Marinate:** 2 hours **Yield:** about ¾ cup (enough for 2 to 2½ pounds meat, poultry, fish, or seafood)

⅓ cup white wine vinegar
¼ cup olive oil or cooking oil
¼ cup white wine
    Worcestershire sauce
1 tablespoon snipped fresh
    tarragon or thyme or
    1 teaspoon dried
    tarragon or thyme,
    crushed
1 tablespoon honey
¼ teaspoon salt
⅛ teaspoon pepper

1 In a small bowl combine vinegar, oil, Worcestershire sauce, tarragon, honey, salt, and pepper. To use, pour marinade over meat, poultry, fish, or seafood in a plastic bag set in a shallow dish; seal bag.

2 Marinate in the refrigerator for 2 to 4 hours for meat or poultry or 1 hour for fish or seafood, turning bag occasionally. Drain, reserving marinade. Smoke meat, poultry, fish, or seafood, brushing once with marinade halfway through cooking. Discard the remaining marinade.

Nutrition Facts per 2 tablespoons: 101 cal., 9 g total fat (1 g sat. fat), 0 mg chol., 182 mg sodium, 5 g carbo., 0 g fiber, 0 g pro.
Daily Values: 1% vit. C, 1% calcium, 1% iron

Citrus Marinade

This refreshing marinade lends a hint of citrus flavor to whatever it touches, without overpowering the natural flavor of the food.

Prep: 5 minutes **Marinate:** 2 hours **Yield:** about ½ cup (enough for about 1½ pounds pork, poultry, fish, or seafood)

¼ cup frozen orange juice
    concentrate, thawed
2 tablespoons cooking oil
2 teaspoons finely shredded
    lemon or lime peel
2 tablespoons lemon or lime
    juice
2 cloves garlic, minced

1 In a small bowl combine juice concentrate, oil, lemon peel, lemon juice, and garlic. To use, pour marinade over pork, poultry, fish, or seafood in a plastic bag set in a shallow dish; seal bag.

2 Marinate in the refrigerator for 2 to 4 hours for pork or poultry or 1 to 2 hours for fish or seafood, turning bag occasionally. Drain, reserving marinade. Smoke pork, poultry, fish, or seafood, brushing once with marinade halfway through cooking. Discard the remaining marinade.

Nutrition Facts per 2 tablespoons: 93 cal., 7 g total fat (1 g sat. fat), 0 mg chol., 1 mg sodium, 8 g carbo., 0 g fiber, 1 g pro.
Daily Values: 1% vit. A, 50% vit. C, 1% calcium, 1% iron

Sides

Hot-Off-the-Grill Potatoes

In This Chapter:

Corn with Ancho-Avocado Butter

Southwestern accents abound in this chile-avocado butter. Ancho peppers are the dried form of the poblano pepper. They're sweet and richly flavored, but not overly hot.

Prep: 25 minutes **Grill:** 25 minutes **Serves:** 6

Butter:

- 2 tablespoons lime juice
- 2 tablespoons water
- ½ to 1 small dried ancho pepper
- 3 tablespoons butter or margarine, softened
- ⅛ teaspoon salt
- ½ of a small avocado, seeded, peeled, and chopped

- 6 fresh ears of corn

1 For butter, in a small saucepan combine lime juice, water, and ancho pepper. Cover and cook over low heat about 10 minutes or until pepper is soft. Drain and cool. Remove stem and seeds from pepper; finely chop pepper. In a small bowl combine pepper, butter, and salt. Slightly mash avocado; stir into butter mixture. Cover and refrigerate until ready to serve.

2 Remove husks and silks from ears of corn. If desired, leave a few leaves of the husks intact.

3 *In a charcoal grill*, grill corn on the rack of an uncovered grill directly over medium coals for 25 to 30 minutes or until corn kernels are tender, turning occasionally. (*In a gas grill*, preheat grill. Reduce heat to medium. Place corn on grill rack over heat. Cover and grill as above.) Serve the corn with butter.

Nutrition Facts per serving: 246 cal., 10 g total fat (2 g sat. fat), 8 mg chol., 125 mg sodium, 40 g carbo., 6 g fiber, 5 g pro.
Daily Values: 10% vit. A, 32% vit. C, 7% iron

Italian Zucchini Boats

These whimsical boats may be all the kids want to eat (a vegetable, no less!). And why not, when the cargo they carry is a heaping helping of smoky bacon, Parmesan cheese, and savory seasonings?

Prep: 20 minutes **Grill:** 8 minutes **Serves:** 8

4 medium-large zucchini
   (6 to 7 ounces each)
Sauce:
2 tablespoons lemon juice
4 teaspoons olive oil
3 large cloves garlic, minced
¼ teaspoon salt
¼ teaspoon pepper

1 recipe Bacon Gremolata

1 Trim ends from zucchini; halve zucchini lengthwise. Hollow out centers with a spoon, removing seeds and forming ¼- to ½-inch-thick shells.

2 For sauce, in a small bowl stir together lemon juice, olive oil, garlic, salt, and pepper. Brush zucchini shells with sauce. Place shells, cut sides down, on a lightly greased grilling tray.

3 *In a charcoal grill*, grill zucchini on tray on the rack of an uncovered grill directly over medium coals for 5 to 7 minutes or until zucchini begins to turn golden. Turn cut sides up and grill for 1 minute. Remove tray from grill. Spoon the Bacon Gremolata into shells, mounding mixture slightly and pressing down lightly. Return to grill. Cover and grill for 2 to 4 minutes more or until cheese begins to melt and zucchini is crisp-tender. (*In a gas grill*, preheat grill. Reduce heat to medium. Place zucchini on tray on grill rack over heat. Cover and grill as above.)

Bacon Gremolata: In a small bowl stir together 8 slices bacon, crisp-cooked, drained, and finely crumbled, or ½ cup finely chopped Canadian-style bacon; ½ cup finely shredded Parmesan cheese; 2 tablespoons snipped fresh basil; 2 tablespoons chopped pepperoncini salad pepper or fresh jalapeño pepper; 2 teaspoons finely shredded lemon peel; 1 clove garlic, minced; and ¼ teaspoon black pepper.

Nutrition Facts per serving: 100 cal., 7 g total fat (3 g sat. fat), 12 mg chol., 306 mg sodium, 4 g carbo., 1 g fiber, 5 g pro.
Daily Values: 8% vit. A, 16% vit. C, 8% calcium, 3% iron

Hot-Off-the-Grill Potatoes

These tasty, foil-packet-prepared potatoes get great flavor from Parmesan cheese, flecks of fresh herbs, and a crumble of crisp bacon. Best of all, they go with anything and require no cleanup.

Prep: 20 minutes **Grill:** 30 minutes **Serves:** 4

3 tablespoons butter
5 medium potatoes
¼ cup chopped green onions
2 tablespoons grated
    Parmesan cheese
¼ teaspoon salt
¼ teaspoon paprika
¼ teaspoon freshly ground
    pepper
3 slices bacon, crisp-cooked,
    drained, and crumbled
2 tablespoons snipped fresh
    parsley
2 tablespoons snipped fresh
    dill
2 tablespoons snipped fresh
    chives

1 Fold a 48×18-inch piece of heavy foil in half to make a 24×18-inch rectangle. Grease with 1 tablespoon of the butter.

2 Scrub and thinly slice unpeeled potatoes. Place potatoes in center of foil. Sprinkle with green onions, Parmesan cheese, salt, paprika, and pepper. Dot with the remaining butter.

3 Bring up 2 opposite edges of foil and seal with a double fold. Fold remaining ends to completely enclose potatoes, leaving space for steam to build.

4 *In a charcoal grill*, grill potato packet on the rack of an uncovered grill directly over medium coals for 30 to 40 minutes or until potatoes are tender, turning packet every 10 minutes during grilling. (*In a gas grill*, preheat grill. Reduce heat to medium. Place potato packet on grill rack over heat. Cover and grill as above.) Before serving, sprinkle potatoes with bacon, parsley, dill, and chives.

Nutrition Facts per serving: 234 cal., 10 g total fat (5 g sat. fat), 22 mg chol., 337 mg sodium, 30 g carbo., 4 g fiber, 7 g pro.
Daily Values: 10% vit. A, 54% vit. C, 6% calcium, 11% iron

Grill-Smoked Mushrooms

Crown a sirloin steak with these smoky mushrooms—and serve it with a blue cheese-topped green salad and hefty chunks of French bread to sop up the delicious, buttery sauce.

Soak: 1 hour **Prep:** 5 minutes **Smoke:** 45 minutes **Serves:** 4 to 6

2 cups hickory or oak wood chips
4 cups thickly sliced or halved fresh mushrooms
¼ cup butter or margarine, cut up
1 teaspoon instant chicken bouillon granules

1 At least 1 hour before smoke cooking, soak wood chips in enough water to cover. Drain before using. In an 8×8×2-inch or 9×9×2-inch baking pan or disposable foil pan combine the mushrooms, butter, and bouillon granules.

2 *In a charcoal grill,* arrange medium-hot coals around edge of grill. Test for medium heat above center of grill. Sprinkle the drained wood chips over the coals. Place mushrooms in pan on the grill rack over center of grill. Cover and smoke for 45 to 60 minutes or until tender, stirring once halfway through cooking. [*In a gas grill,* preheat grill. Reduce heat to medium. Adjust for indirect cooking (see page 6). Smoke as above, except add drained wood chips according to the manufacturer's directions.]

Nutrition Facts per serving: 136 cal., 14 g total fat (8 g sat. fat), 33 mg chol., 344 mg sodium, 3 g carbo., 1 g fiber, 3 g pro.
Daily Values: 9% vit. A, 1% calcium, 3% iron

Mediterranean Salad Platter

Using a colorful assortment of peppers makes this salad lovely to look at and to eat. For a peppery addition to the mix, line the platter with arugula instead of the romaine.

Prep: 15 minutes **Grill:** 10 minutes **Serves:** 10 to 12

8 large red, yellow, and/or green sweet peppers, quartered lengthwise
Romaine leaves
2 large red and/or yellow tomatoes, sliced
2 tablespoons olive oil
1 cup pitted kalamata olives
½ cup crumbled feta cheese (2 ounces)
1 tablespoon snipped fresh tarragon or basil

1 *In a charcoal grill,* grill sweet peppers on the rack of an uncovered grill directly over medium coals about 10 minutes or until peppers are crisp-tender, turning once halfway through grilling. (*In a gas grill,* preheat grill. Reduce heat to medium. Place peppers on grill rack over heat. Cover and grill as above.) Remove from grill. Cut peppers into bite-size strips.

2 Line a serving platter with romaine. Arrange peppers and tomatoes on platter. Drizzle with olive oil; season with salt and pepper. Sprinkle with olives, feta cheese, and tarragon.

Nutrition Facts per serving: 100 cal., 6 g total fat (1 g sat. fat), 5 mg chol., 218 mg sodium, 11 g carbo., 3 g fiber, 2 g pro.
Daily Values: 134% vit. A, 333% vit. C, 4% calcium, 4% iron

Greek Pasta Salad

Feta cheese—a key ingredient in Greek cooking—gets its sharp, salty flavor from the brine in which it is cured.

Prep: 30 minutes **Chill:** 2 hours **Serves:** 6 to 8

6 ounces dried mostaccioli pasta (about 2 cups)
4 plum tomatoes, chopped
½ of a medium cucumber, halved lengthwise and sliced
2 green onions, sliced
3 tablespoons sliced pitted ripe olives

Dressing:
¼ cup olive oil or salad oil
¼ cup lemon juice
1 tablespoon snipped fresh basil or 1 teaspoon dried basil, crushed
1 tablespoon snipped fresh oregano or 1 teaspoon dried oregano, crushed
1 tablespoon anchovy paste (optional)
3 cloves garlic, minced
⅛ teaspoon salt
⅛ teaspoon pepper

½ cup crumbled feta cheese (2 ounces)

1 In a large saucepan cook the pasta in boiling, lightly salted water according to package directions; drain. Rinse with cold water; drain again.

2 In a large bowl toss together the cooked pasta, the tomatoes, cucumber, green onions, and olives.

3 For dressing, in a screw-top jar combine the oil, lemon juice, basil, oregano, anchovy paste (if desired), garlic, salt, and pepper. Cover and shake well. Drizzle over pasta mixture; toss gently to coat.

4 Cover and refrigerate for at least 2 hours or overnight. Before serving, add the feta cheese; toss gently to combine.

Nutrition Facts per serving: 232 cal., 12 g total fat (3 g sat. fat), 8 mg chol., 195 mg sodium, 26 g carbo., 2 g fiber, 6 g pro.
Daily Values: 8% vit. A, 25% vit. C, 7% calcium, 8% iron

The Blues Salad

If you're in the dinnertime doldrums, this fruit-and-greens salad will pick you up in a heartbeat with its harmonious mix of fresh blueberries, blue cheese, and blueberry vinegar.

Prep: 25 minutes **Serves:** 4

Dressing:

¼ cup Blueberry Vinegar, raspberry vinegar, or red wine vinegar

2 tablespoons walnut oil or olive oil

¼ teaspoon salt

¼ teaspoon coarsely ground pepper

4 cups torn mixed salad greens

1 cup fresh blueberries

½ cup walnut halves, toasted

¼ cup crumbled Stilton or other blue cheese

2 tablespoons snipped fresh chives or thinly sliced green onion tops

1 For dressing, in a screw-top jar combine Blueberry Vinegar, walnut oil, salt, and pepper. Cover and shake well.

2 In a large bowl combine salad greens, blueberries, walnuts, Stilton cheese, and chives. Shake dressing and drizzle over greens mixture; toss gently to coat.

Blueberry Vinegar: In a stainless-steel or enamel saucepan combine 2 cups rice vinegar and 1½ cups fresh blueberries. Bring to boiling; reduce heat. Simmer, uncovered, for 3 minutes. Stir in 2 tablespoons honey. Strain through a fine-mesh sieve. Discard berries. Transfer liquid to a clean 1-quart jar or bottle. Add 1½ cups fresh blueberries. Cover tightly with a nonmetallic lid (or cover with plastic wrap and tightly seal with a metal lid). To store vinegar, keep in a cool, dark place up to 6 months. Before using vinegar, discard berries. Makes about 2 cups.

Nutrition Facts per serving: 212 cal., 19 g total fat (3 g sat. fat), 5 mg chol., 254 mg sodium, 9 g carbo., 3 g fiber, 5 g pro.
Daily Values: 13% vit. A, 15% vit. C, 8% calcium, 5% iron

the blues make us happy

I love strong-flavored cheeses, and blue cheese is among my favorites. Blue cheese refers to all types of cheeses that have been treated with molds that make blue or green streaks throughout and impart the cheese with its wonderful flavor. Blue cheeses—including England's Stilton, Italy's Gorgonzola, Iowa's Maytag Blue, France's Roquefort, and Denmark's Danish Blue—vary in degrees of creaminess to crumbliness and strength of flavor and aroma, but I use them in recipes interchangeably.

Colleen Weeden
Test Kitchen Home Economist

Sweets

Chocolate-Walnut Brownie Pudding

In This Chapter:

Little Fruit Tarts

There is something delightful about getting a whole fruit tart to yourself—even if it is petite in stature. Use one kind of fruit or a mix, depending on what's in season.

Prep: 30 minutes **Bake:** 25 minutes **Serves:** 12

Pastry:
- 1½ cups all-purpose flour
- 3 tablespoons sifted powdered sugar
- Dash salt
- ½ cup shortening
- 4 to 6 tablespoons cold water

Filling:
- ¾ cup granulated sugar
- ½ cup all-purpose flour
- Dash almond extract
- 2½ cups fresh fruit (such as raspberries, blackberries, blueberries, gooseberries, quartered strawberries, and/or chopped, peeled apples)

1 For pastry, in a medium bowl stir together the 1½ cups flour, the powdered sugar, and salt. Using a pastry blender, cut in shortening until pieces are pea-size. Sprinkle 1 tablespoon of the water over part of mixture; gently toss with a fork. Push moistened dough to side of bowl. Repeat moistening dough, using 1 tablespoon of the water at a time, until all dough is moistened. Form dough into 12 balls. Press a ball of dough evenly onto the bottom and up the side of each of twelve 2½-inch muffin cups.

2 For filling, in a small bowl combine granulated sugar and the ½ cup flour. Stir in almond extract and enough water (about 3 tablespoons) to make a smooth, thick paste. Divide the fruit among muffin cups. Spoon the almond mixture over fruit.

3 Bake in a 375° oven for 25 to 30 minutes or until the pastry is browned and fruit is tender. Cool in pan on a wire rack. If desired, garnish tarts with additional fresh fruit.

Nutrition Facts per serving: 211 cal., 9 g total fat (2 g sat. fat), 0 mg chol., 12 mg sodium, 31 g carbo., 2 g fiber, 2 g pro.
Daily Values: 1% vit. A, 11% vit. C, 1% calcium, 6% iron

pastry pointers

Homemade pastry isn't difficult to master if you follow a few tips:

• Shortening is the easiest fat to work with when making pastry, but butter will give your pastry a lovely flavor. To work the shortening or butter into the flour, use a pastry blender or two table knives.

• Make sure the water you add is very cold; measure the water from a small bowl of ice water.

• Gently toss the water with the flour mixture just until all the flour mixture is moistened. If the pastry dough is overworked, it may be tough.

Corn Bread Cherry Cobbler

This bubbling dessert features the best flavors the South has to offer—pecans, corn bread, and fresh fruit. It's the perfect ending to a smoked dinner.

Prep: 30 minutes **Bake:** 12 minutes **Serves:** 4

Filling:

- 4 cups pitted tart red cherries or one 16-ounce package frozen unsweetened pitted tart red cherries
- ⅔ cup sugar
- 2 tablespoons cornstarch
- 2 tablespoons orange juice

Biscuit Topping:

- ⅓ cup cornmeal
- 3 tablespoons all-purpose flour
- 1 tablespoon sugar
- 1 tablespoon finely chopped pecans
- ¾ teaspoon baking powder
- 2 tablespoons butter
- 1 slightly beaten egg white
- 1 tablespoon milk

- 1½ teaspoons sugar
- ⅛ teaspoon ground cinnamon
- Half-and-half, light cream, or vanilla ice cream (optional)

1 For filling, in a medium saucepan combine the cherries, the ⅔ cup sugar, the cornstarch, and orange juice. Let fresh cherries stand for 10 minutes or let frozen cherries stand for 20 minutes. Cook and stir mixture over medium heat until thickened and bubbly. Cook and stir for 1 minute more. Reduce heat and keep hot.

2 Meanwhile, for biscuit topping, in a medium bowl stir together the cornmeal, flour, the 1 tablespoon sugar, the pecans, and baking powder. Cut in the butter until the mixture resembles coarse crumbs. In a small bowl combine the egg white and milk. Add all at once to the flour mixture, stirring just until moistened.

3 Spoon the hot fruit mixture into a 1½-quart casserole. Immediately spoon the biscuit topping into 4 or 8 mounds over the hot fruit mixture. Stir together the 1½ teaspoons sugar and the cinnamon. Sprinkle sugar mixture over biscuit mounds.

4 Bake in a 400° oven for 12 to 15 minutes or until a wooden toothpick inserted into the center of a biscuit mound comes out clean. Serve warm. If desired, serve with half-and-half.

Nutrition Facts per serving: 372 cal., 8 g total fat (4 g sat. fat), 17 mg chol., 158 mg sodium, 74 g carbo., 4 g fiber, 4 g pro.
Daily Values: 46% vit. A, 32% vit. C, 8% calcium, 8% iron

Graham Cherry Cobbler: Prepare the Corn Bread Cherry Cobbler as directed, except for biscuit topping omit cornmeal and the 1 tablespoon sugar. Increase the flour to ⅓ cup, add 2 tablespoons finely crushed graham crackers, and 1 tablespoon brown sugar. Increase the milk to 2 tablespoons.

Nutrition Facts per serving: 356 cal., 8 g total fat (4 g sat. fat), 17 mg chol., 175 mg sodium, 69 g carbo., 3 g fiber, 4 g pro.
Daily Values: 45% vit. A, 32% vit. C, 9% calcium, 7% iron

Sticky Peaches and Cream

Amaretti are crisp almond-flavored Italian cookies that are delicious with a cappuccino or in desserts such as this delicious summertime treat.

Prep: 35 minutes **Chill:** 30 minutes **Serves:** 6

2 tablespoons butter

6 ripe medium peaches, peeled, pitted, and sliced, or 6 cups frozen unsweetened peach slices, thawed, drained, and patted dry

2 tablespoons brown sugar

¼ teaspoon ground ginger

6 amaretti cookies or oatmeal cookies

1 recipe Cinnamon Cream

3 tablespoons crumbled amaretti cookies or oatmeal cookies

1 In a large skillet melt butter over medium-high heat. Add peaches. Cook and stir about 2 minutes or until heated through. Sprinkle with brown sugar and ginger. Cook and stir for 1 to 2 minutes more or until peaches are coated and caramelized.

2 Divide the caramelized peaches among 6 dessert bowls. Place the whole amaretti cookies next to peaches. Top with the Cinnamon Cream; sprinkle the peaches with crumbled cookies.

Cinnamon Cream: In a small saucepan combine 3 tablespoons granulated sugar, 2 teaspoons cornstarch, and ¼ teaspoon ground cinnamon. Stir in ½ cup milk. Cook and stir over medium heat until thickened and bubbly. Slowly stir hot mixture into 1 beaten egg yolk. Return mixture to saucepan. Cook and stir about 2 minutes more or until bubbly. Remove from heat. Stir in 2 teaspoons margarine or butter and ½ teaspoon vanilla. Cover surface with plastic wrap; cool without stirring, then cover and refrigerate. Before serving, in a small chilled bowl beat ⅓ cup whipping cream until soft peaks form. Fold whipped cream into chilled mixture. Makes about 1 cup.

Nutrition Facts per serving: 323 cal., 12 g total fat (6 g sat. fat), 66 mg chol., 76 mg sodium, 54 g carbo., 7 g fiber, 4 g pro.
Daily Values: 47% vit. A, 38% vit. C, 6% calcium, 3% iron

Chocolate-Walnut Brownie Pudding

To the unrepentant chocoholic, there is nothing finer than the sweet stuff in its richest, most gooey form. This delectable dessert fills the bill. Ice cream is optimum but not a necessity.

Prep: 15 minutes **Bake:** 40 minutes **Serves:** 6 to 8

1 cup all-purpose flour
¾ cup granulated sugar
2 tablespoons unsweetened cocoa powder
2 teaspoons baking powder
¼ teaspoon salt
½ cup milk
2 tablespoons cooking oil
1 teaspoon vanilla
½ cup chopped walnuts
¾ cup packed brown sugar
¼ cup unsweetened cocoa powder
1½ cups boiling water
Ice cream (optional)

1 Grease an 8×8×2-inch baking pan. Set aside.

2 In a medium bowl stir together the flour, granulated sugar, the 2 tablespoons cocoa powder, the baking powder, and salt. Stir in the milk, oil, and vanilla. Stir in the walnuts. Pour into the prepared pan.

3 In another medium bowl stir together the brown sugar and the ¼ cup cocoa powder. Stir in the boiling water; slowly pour over batter in pan.

4 Bake in a 350° oven for 40 minutes. Serve warm. If desired, serve with ice cream.

Nutrition Facts per serving: 406 cal., 12 g total fat (2 g sat. fat), 2 mg chol., 254 mg sodium, 70 g carbo., 1 g fiber, 6 g pro.
Daily Values: 1% vit. A, 1% vit. C, 20% calcium, 13% iron

Citrus-Hazelnut Bars

This elegant cookie ups the ante on the much-beloved lemon bar. A homemade orange-lemon curd makes a creamy filling between a layer of buttery, hazelnut-flavored pastry and nuggets of toasted nuts.

Prep: 15 minutes **Bake:** 30 minutes **Serves:** 20

Crust:
- ⅓ cup butter
- ¼ cup granulated sugar
- 1 cup all-purpose flour
- 3 tablespoons finely chopped toasted hazelnuts (filberts) or chopped almonds

Filling:
- 2 eggs
- ¾ cup granulated sugar
- 2 tablespoons all-purpose flour
- 1 teaspoon finely shredded orange peel
- 2 tablespoons orange juice
- 1 teaspoon finely shredded lemon peel
- 1 tablespoon lemon juice
- ½ teaspoon baking powder

- 3 tablespoons finely chopped toasted hazelnuts (filberts) or chopped almonds
- Powdered sugar (optional)

1 For crust, in a medium bowl beat the butter with an electric mixer on medium to high speed for 30 seconds. Add the ¼ cup granulated sugar. Beat until thoroughly combined. Beat in the 1 cup flour and 3 tablespoons nuts until mixture is crumbly.

2 Press mixture onto the bottom of an ungreased 8×8×2-inch baking pan. Bake in a 350° oven about 10 minutes or until lightly browned.

3 Meanwhile, for filling, in a small bowl stir together the eggs, the ¾ cup granulated sugar, the 2 tablespoons flour, the orange peel, orange juice, lemon peel, lemon juice, and baking powder. Beat on medium speed about 2 minutes or until combined. Pour over hot baked layer. Sprinkle with 3 tablespoons nuts.

4 Bake about 20 minutes more or until the edges are lightly browned and center is set. Cool in pan on a wire rack. If desired, sift powdered sugar over top. Cut into bars. To store, cover and refrigerate.

Nutrition Facts per serving: 112 cal., 5 g total fat (2 g sat. fat), 30 mg chol., 50 mg sodium, 15 g carbo., 0 g fiber, 2 g pro.
Daily Values: 3% vit. A, 3% vit. C, 1% calcium, 3% iron

Toasted Almond Ice Cream

You just can't buy ice cream like this—not even the gourmet sort that's a cut above the rest. This is the real thing: rich, creamy, and resplendent with toasted almonds.

Prep: 30 minutes **Chill:** 1 hour **Ripen:** 4 hours **Serves:** 12

½ cup sugar
2 cups milk
2 cups whipping cream
½ cup sugar
4 slightly beaten egg yolks
½ teaspoon almond extract
¾ to 1 cup toasted almonds,
      chopped
   Fresh raspberries
      (optional)
   Chocolate ice-cream
      topping (optional)

1 In a heavy medium saucepan cook ½ cup sugar over medium-high heat until sugar begins to melt, shaking the saucepan occasionally to heat the sugar evenly. Do not stir. Once the sugar starts to melt, reduce heat to low and cook about 5 minutes more or until all of the sugar is melted and golden, stirring as needed with a wooden spoon. Remove from heat.

2 In a small saucepan heat the milk just until bubbles form around edge of liquid. Do not allow to boil. Gradually stir warmed milk into melted sugar. Cook and stir over medium heat until sugar is dissolved. Remove from heat.

3 In a medium bowl combine whipping cream, ½ cup sugar, and egg yolks. Stir in 1 cup of the warmed milk mixture. Return to saucepan. Cook and stir over medium heat just until mixture comes to a boil. Transfer to bowl. Stir in almond extract. Cover and refrigerate for 1 to 2 hours or until completely cooled.

4 Freeze in a 4- to 5-quart ice-cream freezer according to the manufacturer's directions. Stir in almonds. Ripen for 4 hours. If desired, garnish each serving with raspberries and topping.

Nutrition Facts per serving: 290 cal., 21 g total fat (11 g sat. fat), 128 mg chol., 61 mg sodium, 22 g carbo., 1 g fiber, 5 g pro.
Daily Values: 30% vit. A, 1% vit. C, 8% calcium, 3% iron

toasting nuts, seeds, and coconut

Whether you're toasting nuts, seeds, or coconut—all of which get heightened flavor and crunch from some time in the oven—the process is the same. Simply spread out whatever is to be toasted in a single layer in a shallow pan. Bake in a 350° oven for 5 to 10 minutes, stirring once or twice, until golden brown and fragrant. Let cool before using.

INDEX

Photographs indicated in **bold**.

Metric Cooking Hints

By making a few conversions, cooks in Australia, Canada, and the United Kingdom can use the recipes in this book with confidence. The charts on this page provide a guide for converting measurements from the U.S. customary system, which is used throughout this book, to the imperial and metric systems. There also is a conversion table for oven temperatures to accommodate the differences in oven calibrations.

Product Differences: Most of the ingredients called for in the recipes in this book are available in English-speaking countries. However, some are known by different names. Here are some common U.S. American ingredients and their possible counterparts:
● Sugar is granulated or castor sugar.
● Powdered sugar is icing sugar.
● All-purpose flour is plain household flour or white flour. When self-rising flour is used in place of all-purpose flour in a recipe that calls for leavening, omit the leavening agent (baking soda or baking powder) and salt.
● Light-colored corn syrup is golden syrup.
● Cornstarch is cornflour.
● Baking soda is bicarbonate of soda.
● Vanilla is vanilla essence.
● Green, red, or yellow sweet peppers are capsicums.
● Golden raisins are sultanas.

Volume and Weight: U.S. Americans traditionally use cup measures for liquid and solid ingredients. The chart, above right, shows the approximate imperial and metric equivalents. If you are accustomed to weighing solid ingredients, the following approximate equivalents will help:
● 1 cup butter, castor sugar, or rice = 8 ounces = about 230 grams
● 1 cup flour = 4 ounces = about 115 grams
● 1 cup icing sugar = 5 ounces = about 140 grams

Spoon measures are used for smaller amounts of ingredients. Although the size of the tablespoon varies slightly in different countries, for practical purposes and for recipes in this book, a straight substitution is all that's necessary.

Measurements made using cups or spoons always should be level unless stated otherwise.

Equivalents: U.S. = Australia/U.K.

⅛ teaspoon = 1 ml
¼ teaspoon = 1.25 ml
½ teaspoon = 2.5 ml
1 teaspoon = 5 ml
1 tablespoon = 15 ml
1 fluid ounce = 30 ml
¼ cup = 60 ml
⅓ cup = 80 ml
½ cup = 120 ml
⅔ cup = 160 ml
¾ cup = 180 ml
1 cup = 240 ml
2 cups = 475 ml
1 quart = 1 liter
½ inch = 1.25 cm
1 inch = 2.5 cm

Baking Pan Sizes

U.S. American	Metric
8×1½-inch round baking pan	20×4-cm cake tin
9×1½-inch round baking pan	23×4-cm cake tin
11×7×1½-inch baking pan	28×18×4-cm baking tin
13×9×2-inch baking pan	32×23×5-cm baking tin
2-quart rectangular baking dish	28×18×4-cm baking tin
15×10×1-inch baking pan	38×25.5×2.5-cm baking tin (Swiss roll tin)
9-inch pie plate	22×4- or 23×4-cm pie plate
7- or 8-inch springform pan	18- or 20-cm springform or loose-bottom cake tin
9×5×3-inch loaf pan	23×13×8-cm or 2-pound narrow loaf tin or pâté tin
1½-quart casserole	1.5-liter casserole
2-quart casserole	2-liter casserole

Oven Temperature Equivalents

Fahrenheit Setting	Celsius Setting*	Gas Setting
300°F	150°C	Gas Mark 2 (very low)
325°F	170°C	Gas Mark 3 (low)
350°F	180°C	Gas Mark 4 (moderate)
375°F	190°C	Gas Mark 5 (moderately hot)
400°F	200°C	Gas Mark 6 (hot)
425°F	220°C	Gas Mark 7 (hot)
450°F	230°C	Gas Mark 8 (very hot)
475°F	240°C	Gas Mark 9 (very hot)
Broil		Grill

*Electric and gas ovens may be calibrated using Celsius. However, for an electric oven, increase the Celsius setting 10 to 20 degrees when cooking above 160°C. For convection or forced-air ovens (gas or electric), lower the temperature setting 10°C when cooking at all heat levels.